Primary Language

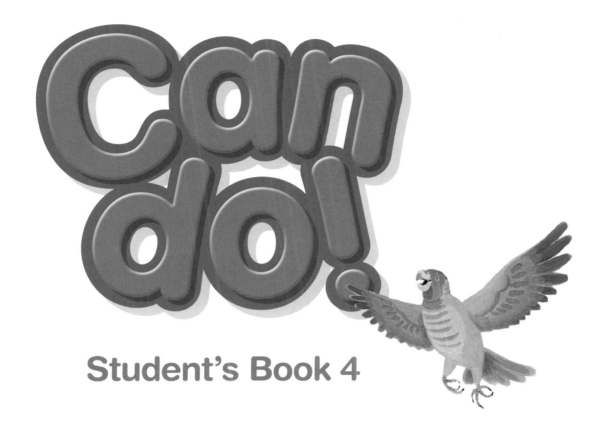

Can do!

Student's Book 4

Project Co-ordinator Angela Mariatte

Lisa Charlemagne   Leona Bastien   Sharlize Anthony   Sylvie Edward
Zenith Edward   Nadezahe Lucien   Carla Alexander   Mathilda Samuel
Williamson Beharry   Vernetta Paul   Jennifer Popo

macmillan
education

Contents

Introduction

The **CAN DO!** Series is the revised edition of what were known as the 'CLAP books', but commonly referred to as the 'CAMDU books'. This revised edition responds to the wishes of the teachers and the needs of the students. Teachers were keen that it should be an integrated Language Arts text. The skills of listening and speaking, reading and writing are therefore incorporated in the units, providing practice activities for students to improve and extend their Language Arts. For the first time, listening scripts are included to provide speaking models and standards for students.

For each of the Grades from Kindergarten through to Grade 6, the new edition now consists of a Student's Book and a Workbook instead of the three previous texts of Reader, Workbook and Activity Book. In addition, a Teacher's Handbook will accompany each level.

The new CAN DO! texts were developed in collaboration with classroom teachers who wrote new material or revised the existing texts. It is a labour of love by experienced educators providing rich and relevant activities in listening, speaking, reading and writing to enrich the practice of standard English. Phonics activities provide opportunities for reading and writing, particularly in Grades K and 1. The narrative passages reflect our rich cultural heritage in the stories of Compere Lapin and Brer Anansi and the expository texts provide for the integration of Science and Social Studies. The Review units at the start of each Student's Book 1 to 6 remind students of the Language Arts they have already learnt at the start of their new school year, and the subsequent Revision units provide for consolidation of new learning at regular stages throughout the year.

The new series has developed into a delightful and lively programme with vibrant photographs, illustrations, graphs and charts that portray our Caribbean culture. My gratitude goes to the teachers who worked tirelessly to write and revise the original books. My deepest appreciation is extended to the persons whose photographs were used and the photographers for an excellent job. To the classroom teachers, I implore you to make effective use of the texts, integrating them into the curriculum to provide our children with rich and rewarding experiences in the classroom and beyond.

Many thanks to the Macmillan team for their professional guidance.

Angela Mariatte (Project Co-ordinator)
Curriculum Specialist, Language Arts

Scope and Sequence

Unit	Listening and speaking	Reading and comprehension	Language	Writing
	**Review: Reading** Realistic story: *The New Library* **Language:** Revise parts of speech, simple present and past tenses, capital letters, synonyms **Writing:** Book report			
1	Listen to and discuss presentation	**Friendly letter:** Letter of invitation SKILL: Surveying	Noun types: common, proper, collective, abstract Alphabetical order	Friendly letter **WRITING PROCESS:** Planning
2	Phone dialogue inviting friend to event	**Expository text:** *Flower Festivals* SKILL: Predicting	Sentence structure and punctuation, subject and predicate, subject–verb agreement *am/is/are*	Report about an event **WRITING PROCESS:** Getting ideas, drafting
3	Listen to, retell story, suggest new ending	**Realistic story:** *A Match to Remember* SKILL: Skimming Story structure	Review simple past tense: regular/irregular verbs, *was/were* Questions, negatives Sequencing words	Write a new story ending
4	Listen to biography, give presentation	**Biography:** *Lightning Bolt* SKILL: Scanning Complete a timeline	Pronouns Root words, syllables	STUDY SKILL: Make notes Write a biography
5	Listen to and discuss poem *The Hen*	**Poem:** *The Donkey* Rhyme, rhythm, alliteration	Adjectives: comparative and superlative Suffixes forming adjectives	Description of an animal using a web to plan
6	Listen to a radio announcement, create own announcement	**Environmental text:** Invitation, schedule, advertisement Fact and opinion	Future tense, possessive adjectives and pronouns Abbreviations	Create a poster advertising a product
	**Revision 1: Reading** Letter to a friend **Language:** noun types, subject–verb agreement, simple past tense, past tense, comparative/superlative adjectives, pronouns **Words:** alphabetical order, root words, syllables, suffixes, abbreviations **Writing:** Friendly letter			
7	Listen to a radio announcement, create own announcement	**Traditional story:** *Monkey and Alligator* SKILL: Story structure	Quotation marks **Study skill:** Using a dictionary	Story plan Write story about a problem
8	Presentation from a resource person	**Expository text:** *Our Forests*	Present continuous tense Synonyms and antonyms	Paragraphing: Main idea, supporting details
9	Listen to and discuss poem *Waves*	**Realistic story:** *Sea Adventure*	Adverbs: Comparative and superlative Similes, personification	Description of a place
10	Listen to and record information, discuss student presentation	**Expository text:** Computers SKILL: Using a website	Conjunctions: *and, but, so, because, although* Suffixes forming nouns	Report about an invention

Unit	Listening and speaking	Reading and comprehension	Language	Writing
11	Listen to realistic story Review story	**Realistic story:** *Computer Brain* Cause and effect	Possessive nouns Prefixes	Letter of thanks Apply writing process
12	Dialogue about school uniform Conduct debate	**Formal letter:** Request for Dress Down Day Formal/informal language	Using commas in lists and addresses First conditional Homophones	Formal letter of request

Revision 2: Reading *The King's Watchman* **Language:** quotation marks, present continuous tense, conjunctions *and, but, so*, possessive nouns, adverbs **Words:** prefixes, synonyms, antonyms, homophones **Study Skills:** using a dictionary **Writing:** Story based on proverb

Unit	Listening and speaking	Reading and comprehension	Language	Writing
13	Listen to, discuss presentation	**Expository text:** *Reptiles in Saint Lucia* KWL strategy	Articles: *a/an/the some/any* STUDY SKILLS: Table of contents Index	Report about an animal
14	Listen to, discuss fire drill	**Leaflet:** *Fire Safety*	Instructions Indefinite pronouns Negative words Homographs	Write instructions for fire safety
15	News report, describe a scene	**Realistic story:** *Bamboo Bursting* Discuss character	Present perfect tense Relative pronouns Context	Picture story
16	Listen to, discuss announcement about waste	**Graphic information:** Waste: table and pie chart	Colons Prepositions Compound nouns	Summarise graphic information
17	Listen to and discuss radio call-in programme	**Poem:** *Our Homeland* Onomatopoeia	Past continuous tense with simple past tense SKILL: Using a thesaurus	Write an acrostic
18	Listen to and role play first part of story	**Drama:** *Ti Jean and Jablotin* Features of a play	Contractions *it's/its* *there/their/they're* Interjections	Write dialogue for a play

Revision 3: Reading: Expository text on volcanoes; *Anansi and the Tug-of-War* **Language:** present perfect, past continuous, contractions, prepositions, joining sentences: with relative pronouns *which, who, where*, and conjunctions *because, although* **Words:** homophones, compound nouns **Study Skills:** graphs, using a thesaurus **Writing:** Factual report, story

Review

Before you read: Look at the picture.
What is the student doing? What do you think the story will be about?

The New Library

The students at Palm View Primary School love reading but there were not many books in their school library. Last year a student from the school, Tanice Paul, won first prize in the Nations Bookstore Reading Competition. The manager of the bookstore donated books to the school.

Mrs. Williams, the school principal, decided to build a new library at the school. When the building was completed, the Grade Six students helped to paint the walls. Some of the parents built shelves for the books. A former student from the school, Mr. Johnson, donated two new computers to the library.

The students were excited when the new library opened. Mrs. Williams chose Tanice and Kirk to be library monitors. They help Mrs. James, the librarian, and they show new students how to find the books they want.

One day, Mr. Johnson came to visit. Tanice took him on a tour of the library. First she showed him the fiction section.

"This is where we keep story books, plays and poems," she told him.

Then they went to the reference section. "This is where we go to find out information," Tanice said.

"How often do you come to the library?" Mr. Johnson asked.

"Every class comes here once a week," said Tanice. "We have Library Club three times a week, so some of us come here more often."

"What do you do in Library Club?" asked Mr. Johnson.

"Mrs. James, the librarian, reads us stories. She is very kind. She helps us with our projects and shows us how to use the computers."

"Can you take books out of the library?"

"Yes, we can borrow a book for a week," replied Tanice. "If we bring it back late, we have to pay a fine."

"Thank you for showing me around your library, Tanice," said Mr. Johnson. "I am glad that you like using it."

Comprehension

1 Why did the principal decide to build a new library?
2 Who helped to get the new library ready? What did they do?
3 Which person was once a student at Palm View Primary School?
   a Mrs. James   **b** the bookstore manager   **c** Mr. Johnson
4 In which section of the library can you find story books?
5 Where do you go to find out information?
6 A librarian is a person who
   a borrows books from a library. **b** uses the computers in the library.
   c looks after the books in a library.
7 What is a *fine*?
8 Do you think going to the library is important? Why?

Language   Parts of speech

1 **Match the parts of speech with their definitions.**

adjective   a short word which replaces a noun
noun   an action word
pronoun   a word which names people, animals, places and things
verb   a word which tells us more about a noun

2 **Find four examples of each part of speech in the story.**

Adjectives	Nouns	Pronouns	Verbs
new			

3 List five or more nouns, verbs and adjectives. Use your own ideas.
Example: Nouns: town, shop, …

Singular and plural

Write the plural forms of the following nouns.

1 book books	**5** story	**9** match
2 shelf	**6** class	**10** potato
3 library	**7** child	**11** brush
4 man	**8** box	**12** bus

Verbs

1 Choose the correct verbs to complete the sentences.

1 The students (**goes** / **go**) to the library once a week.
2 The librarian (**lets** / **let**) students borrow books.
3 Tanice and Kirk (**tidies** / **tidy**) the library at the end of the day.
4 Students who (**brings** / **bring**) books back late (**has** / **have**) to pay a fine.
5 I always (**asks** / **ask**) my sister to help me with my projects.
6 If you (**wants** / **want**) to borrow a book, you must ask the librarian.

2 Complete the sentences with the simple past tense forms of the verbs.

borrowed
1 I (**borrow**) a book from the library yesterday.
2 We all (**help**) to paint the classroom walls.
3 It (**take**) a long time for the paint to dry.
4 Kirk (**tell**) me where to find the book I wanted.
5 We (**go**) on a class outing last week.
6 We (**eat**) our lunch under the trees.
7 I (**write**) about the visit in my exercise book.
8 We all (**have**) a really good time.

Punctuation

Rewrite these sentences using capital letters where they are needed.

1 mr. johnson visited palm view school.
2 kirk bought a book at the nations' book store.
3 the teacher was very pleased with tara's work.
4 we all went to castries on sunday.
5 in december, we will have our christmas holiday.
6 my cousin from america will visit us next week.

Revise singular and plural nouns, simple present and past tense verbs, capital letters.

Words Synonyms

1 **Choose synonyms from the list below to replace the underlined words.**

> pleased   finished   silent   assist   tidy   anxious

1 We must be <u>quiet</u> in a library.
2 Tanice's work is always very <u>neat</u>.
3 The students were <u>delighted</u> with their new library.
4 Greg was <u>worried</u> because he could not find his books.
5 When the building was <u>completed</u>, the students painted the walls.
6 Tanice and Kirk <u>help</u> in the school library.

2 **Make new words by joining the words in the box to the suffixes.**

Example: care + ful = *careful*

care help sun self fool noise	-y -ful
thirst thought	-less -ish

3 **Choose four of the words you made and write them in sentences.**

Writing Book report

⭐ **TASK:** **Write a report on a book or story you read last term or during the holidays.**

1 **Copy the table and make notes.**

Do not retell the whole story. Note two or three important events in the story.

Name of story	
Where it is set	
Characters in story	
What happens	
What I like about the story	

2 **Write your report.**
- Check it carefully to see that it makes sense.
- Remember to write in full sentences.

Listening and Speaking

1 **Look at the picture. Discuss the questions.**
- Where are the people in the picture?
- Why do you think they are there?

2 **Listen to Kim's presentation. Answer the questions.**
- What did you learn about her holiday?
- How do you think she felt about the holiday?
- What questions would you like to ask Kim?

3 **Work in pairs. Tell each other what you did during your holidays.**

Reading

Before you read: Survey the text below.
Why is Rufus writing to Mervin?

> **Surveying** means looking over a text to see what type of text it is, and what it is about.

12 High Street,
New Gardens,
Saint Lucia.
11th October, 2016

Dear Mervin,

   I know that you will be surprised to get this letter as I have not written for sometime. Mum says that I can invite you to stay with us in Saint Lucia during the holidays. I am so excited that I can hardly wait to see you.

We have so many interesting activities planned for you. First, we will visit the Sulphur Springs. This is the world's only drive-in volcano. You will see bubbling pools of hot water and steam rising from the ground there. You can actually smell the sulphur; it smells like rotten eggs. However, people say that the gas is beneficial for your health.

The botanical gardens and the mineral baths are near the Sulphur Springs. The baths were built by the French King Louis XV for his soldiers around three hundred years ago. The water in the baths is warm as it comes from a hot spring. We can take a dip in the baths if you like.

One day, we will travel to the north of the island to visit Pigeon Point. There is an old military fort built there when the French and the British were fighting over Saint Lucia. We can take a stroll to the top of the fort. There, you can see Martinique in the distance on a fine day.

On the way home, we can go shopping at the Bay Walk Mall in Gros Islet or visit the shopping centres in Castries. My mother will treat us to pizza at a restaurant after we finish shopping.

When you arrive, we will meet you at Hewanorra International Airport. It is in the south of the island near Vieux Fort town. From there it is quite a long journey to Castries, but the road goes through the mountains and the rainforest. I know you will enjoy the beautiful scenery on the way.

Please give my best wishes to Uncle John and Aunt Grace. I hope they will let you come and stay.

Your cousin,
Rufus

1 Give the names of two places Rufus intends to visit with his cousin.
2 What will the boys see at the drive-in volcano?
3 In the sentence 'The gas is beneficial for your health', what is the meaning of *beneficial*?

   a good   **b** happy   **c** harmful
4 How old are the mineral baths?
5 Which two countries fought over Saint Lucia?
6 What will the boys do after visiting Pigeon Point?
7 Where will Mervin arrive when he comes to Saint Lucia?
8 Which other places would you visit if you had cousins staying with you?

Language   Nouns

Common and proper nouns

> **Nouns** are names given to people, animals, places and things.
> **Common nouns** are general names: cousin, donkey, airport, plane
> **Proper nouns** are special names: Mervin, Castries, Saint Lucia
> Proper nouns begin with a capital letter.

1 Find four common nouns and four proper nouns in Rufus' letter.

2 Find the common and proper nouns in the paragraph below. Copy and complete the table.

During the holidays, Rufus' cousin Mervin came to stay. The plane landed at Hewanorra International Airport. The family took a taxi from Vieux Fort to Castries. Mervin stayed for two weeks. The boys went to the beach every day. One day Rufus' mother took them to Soufrière to see the Pitons. Afterwards they walked in the rainforest and saw some parrots. Mervin had a great time in Saint Lucia.

Common nouns	Proper nouns
holidays	Rufus

Collective nouns

> **Collective** nouns name groups of people, animals and things.
> a flock of birds – a number of birds together
> a swarm of bees – a number of bees together
> Flock and swarm are collective nouns.

3 **Match the collective nouns with the groups they describe.**

Example: *a litter of kittens*

a litter	students
a choir	goats
a class	kittens
a bunch	sailors
a herd	singers
a shoal	plates
a set	flowers
a crew	fish

4 **Complete each sentence with a collective noun from the list below.**

bouquet   team   flight   crew   chest   pack   crowd   clump

1 There was a _____ of people at the shopping mall.
2 A long _____ of steps leads to the fort.
3 Mervin put his things in the _____ of drawers.
4 Uncle John gave Mum a beautiful _____ of flowers.
5 The boys went to see the Saint Lucian cricket _____ play.
6 We spotted the parrot in the _____ of trees.
7 A _____ of dogs roams the street at nights.
8 The air _____ looked after the passengers during the flight.

Abstract nouns

> **Abstract nouns** refer to qualities which we cannot touch, hear, taste, or smell.
> Rufus is my <u>friend</u>. (*Friend* is a common noun.)
> Our <u>friendship</u> is important to us. (*Friendship* is an abstract noun.)

5 **Which of the following nouns are abstract nouns?**

kindness   parent   honesty   silence   island   ocean   beauty   storm

5 Find the abstract nouns in the sentences below.

1 Mervin was impressed by the beauty of the island. *beauty*
2 There is no danger when you visit the Sulphur Springs.
3 It was fun bathing in the mineral pools.
4 You need a lot of patience when you go fishing.
5 On the last day, Rufus' mother had a surprise for the boys.
6 Kim took great pride in her new camera.
7 Mrs. Samuel asked her students to show respect for one another.
8 We should always tell the truth if we do something wrong

6 Identify the noun type for each group. Which noun is the odd one out?

Example: plane   airport   Canada   tourist
Noun type: Common   Odd one out: Canada

1 Castries	Barbados	Caribbean	islands
2 swarm	goats	shoal	bunch
3 mother	children	kindness	uncle
4 freedom	champion	courage	hope
5 pilot	fisherman	flock	driver
6 America	Europe	Africa	continent

Study Skills   Alphabetical order

Words are listed in **alphabetical order** in sources of information such as dictionaries, indexes or directories. If two words begin with the same letter, we use the second or third letters to put them in alphabetical order: **ba**ck, **be**at, **bo**ok, **br**ush

1 Which word would come first in a dictionary?

1 island garden	4 shopping snack	7 trail trader
2 steam spring	5 scenery sunshine	8 bloom blossom
3 water wind	6 flower floor	9 screen scream

2 Put these words in alphabetical order.

1 mountain	rainforest	volcano	river
2 Grenada	Barbados	Antigua	Saint Lucia
3 Mervin	Rufus	Luke	Kayla
4 beach	bird	ball	book
5 church	child	chain	chocolate

We write **friendly letters** for different reasons, e.g. to give our news, to thank someone, to invite someone to an event, to apologise.
A friendly letter has five parts.
Heading: writer's address and the date of the letter
Greeting: Dear + the name of the person to whom you are writing.
Body: the main part of the letter
Closing: We use words such as Love, Your friend, Your niece in the closing
Signature: The name of the person writing the letter.

Study the layout for a friendly letter. Name the five parts.

Example: *1 Heading*

(1) _____
_____
_____

_____ (2)
(3) _____
_____
_____
_____

(4) _____
(5) _____

⭐ **TASK: Write a letter to a friend. Invite him or her to spend the day with you.**
- Tell your friend what you plan to do.
- Say where you will meet and when.

1 **Discuss your plans for the day with another student.**

2 **Write your letter. Remember to:**
- use the correct layout for a friendly letter.
- write in full sentences.
- check your letter carefully for spelling and grammar before you give it to your teacher.

Listening and Speaking

1 **Work in pairs. Look at the picture and discuss the questions.**
- Which cultural event does it show?
- Which cultural activity do you enjoy most? Why?

2 **Listen to the phone conversation.**
- Why is Shanice phoning her friend?
- What information does she give her?

3 **Work in pairs. Role play a phone conversation.**
- Imagine that you are inviting a friend to take part in a cultural event.
- Describe this event to your friend and say what you will do.

Predicting means using clues such as titles and pictures to help you think what a text will be about.

Reading

Before you read: Predict what you will read about in this text.

The flower festivals of La Rose and La Marguerite are unique to Saint Lucia. You will not find them on any other Caribbean island. These festivals combine the cultures of the different people who have lived on the island: British, French and African.

The Festival of La Rose is celebrated on 30th August each year. Saint Rose of Lima is the patron saint of the festival and the rose flower is the symbol of the La Rose Society. The Festival of La Marguerite takes place on 17th October, the feast day of Saint Marguerite, the patron saint of the La Marguerite Society. The marguerite flower is the symbol of this society.

Each society is like a small kingdom. It has different characters which include a king, a queen, and princes and princesses. There are many other characters, such as a governor, magistrates, doctors and nurses, soldiers and policemen. Each society has its own laws, and those who break them have to pay a fine.

Before the festival, each society holds *séances* where members feast and dance and practise their festival songs, which are sung in Creole. In the songs, each society praises the beauty of its flower, saying that it is more beautiful than the flower of the other group.

On the day of the festival, the king of the society wears a crown and a suit decorated with gold and silver medals which shine in the sun. The queen wears a magnificent dress and carries a sceptre and an orb. The La Rose characters wear brightly coloured costumes in gold, pink and red. Those of La Marguerite wear blue, purple, white and silver.

Each flower festival begins with a church service. Then members of the society parade through the streets singing their festival songs. The singing is led by a *chantwelle*. Everyone joins in the chorus, singing either 'Vive la Rose' or 'Vive la Marguerite'.

In the evening there is a *grande fête* during which the characters act out their roles. The king and queen rule over the members. The soldiers and policemen guard the kingdom. The magistrate tries those who have broken the law, while the doctors and nurses care for the sick. The celebration ends with a grand dinner or dance.

Comprehension

1 How many different cultures are represented in the Flower Festivals?

2 The word *unique* means

    a not found anywhere else **b** found in a lot of places **c** not very interesting

3 What are the dates of the flower festivals in Saint Lucia?

4 Which characters do you think would arrest people who break the law of the societies?

5 What happens at a *séance*?

6 What do the societies sing about in their festival songs?

7 Are the following statements true or false?

    a The king of each society carries a sceptre and an orb.

    b A *chantwelle* is a person who sings.

    c The festival songs are sung in French.

    d There is a church service before the parade.

8 Which character would you like to play? Why?

Language Sentences

Sentence types

Sentences are groups of words which make sense. They must have both a subject and a verb. The subject is the person or thing which does the action.

The members practise their festival songs.

subject   verb

A **phrase** is part of a sentence. It does not make sense on its own.

their festival songs → phrase

1 Which of the following are sentences? Which are phrases?

1 The members sing songs in Creole.

2 Wear brightly coloured costumes.

3 The festival begins with a church service.

4 The king's silver medals shine in the sun.

5 More beautiful than the other flower.

6 Before the festival.

2 Use the phrases in Exercise 1 in sentences.

Answer comprehension questions. / Sentence types and punctuation

There are several different types of sentences.
Statement: The king of the society wears a crown.
Question: When is the Festival of La Rose?
Instruction: Turn right at the crossroads.
Exclamation: Hurry up! That's amazing!

3 **Read the sentences. Identify the sentence type.**

1 Would you like to come to the festival with me?
2 What a surprise!
3 Meet me at the bus stop in ten minutes.
4 Dana took pictures of the parade.
5 Shanice invited Dana to come to the parade.
6 Bring a bottle of water with you.

Sentences always begin with a capital letter.
Statements and **instructions** end with a full stop.
Questions end with a question mark. ?
Exclamations end with an exclamation mark. !

4 **Write these sentences correctly.**

1 we will all join in the singing
2 do you know any Creole songs
3 there will be a feast after the parade
4 what a magnificent sight
5 when will we go home
6 be quiet mummy has a headache

Subject and predicate

Every sentence is made up of a subject and predicate.
The subject of the sentence performs the action.
The predicate is the other part of the sentence. It contains the verb.

Subject	Predicate
The king and queen	rule over the members.
Everyone	sang the festival songs.

5 **Read the sentences. Copy and complete the table.**

1   The rose is my favourite flower.
2   My friends and I wore colourful costumes.
3   Shanice and Dana went to the parade yesterday.
4   We practised our songs for the festival.
5   The dancers and the musicians joined the parade.
6   I told my grandparents about the feast.

Subject	Predicate
1 The rose	is my favourite flower.

Subject–verb agreement

> Verbs must agree with their subjects. If the subject is singular (one person or thing), we use a **singular verb**.
> The queen wears a magnificent dress.
> subject ⌐ verb
> For plural subjects, we use a **plural verb**. The girls love the costumes.
> subject ⌐ verb

1 **Write the subjects of the following sentences. State whether they are singular or plural.**

1   Shanice goes to the parade each year. *Shanice, singular*
2   The children dance to the music.
3   My brother and sister play in a band.
4   Our teacher can sing really well.
5   We always take part in the Rose Festival.
6   Most of the students in my class are in the school choir.

2 **Choose the correct verb forms to complete the paragraph**

loves

My brother Tim (1 **loves** / **love**) music. He (2 **goes** / **go**) to music lessons with his friend Josh. They (3 **plays** / **play**) the trumpet in a band. My mother often (4 **helps** / **help**) Tim with his music. Sometimes Tim and Josh (5 **takes** / **take**) part in a parade. My parents always (6 **watches** / **watch**) the parade. After the parade they sometimes (7 **buys** / **buy**) ice cream for the boys before they (8 **comes** / **come**) home. Tim (9 **wants** / **want**) to learn to play the guitar next year. His teacher (10 **thinks** / **think**) he is good at music.

> The verb *be* has three different forms: *am, is, are.*
>
> I am   you are   he/she is   we are   they are

3 Complete the sentences with *am, is* or *are.*

1 My friend and I ____ both nine years old.
2 My grandparents ____ always very kind to me.
3 Dana ____ very excited about the festival.
4 I ____ not able to go to the parade with you.
5 The dancers ____ very tired now.
6 The music ____ very loud.

Writing   Report

⭐ **TASK:** Write about an event you attend every year, such as Independence Day celebrations or Carnival.

1 Get ideas for your report. Copy the table and note your ideas.

Name of event	
When it takes place	
Where	
What happens	
Why I enjoy the event	

2 Note down words you could use in your report.

Examples: music   dancing   costumes   exciting

3 Write a first draft of your report.
- Show your draft to another student.
- Ask this student to say what he or she likes about your draft and to suggest how you could make it better.

> A *draft* is the first version of a piece of writing which you can change and improve.

4 Revise your first draft.
- Make improvements then read it through to be sure that it makes sense.
- Check the spelling and punctuation.

Listening and Speaking

1 **Look at the picture. What do you think is happening?**

2 **Listen to the story.**

Were your predictions about the picture correct? What was different?

3 **Work in pairs.**

* Retell the story.
* What do you think happened next? Continue the story.
* Tell the next part of your story to another student pair.

Compare your stories. What is the same about them? What is different?

Reading

> **Skimming** is looking quickly over a text to get a general idea of what it is about.

Before you read: Skim the story.

Who are the main characters?   Where is the story set?

A Match to Remember

Bel-Air Primary School had won Primary Schools' Football Tournament for the past two years. They were determined to win the trophy for the third time. One of their best players was Brandon, the goalkeeper. Brandon was in a class of his own. He never let a goal through.

On the day of the tournament. Brandon was late for breakfast. His mother went upstairs to check on him. He was still in bed. His head was buried under the bedclothes and he was shivering. Brandon's mother put her hand on his forehead. It was burning hot. Brandon would not be able to play that day.

When Kim, Brandon's twin sister, learnt of his illness, she burst into tears. She knew that the team depended on him. She ran to school to give the sports coach the bad news. The news of Brandon's illness spread like wildfire. Staff and students alike were disappointed. They knew that no one could replace Brandon in goal.

The sports coach chose Martin to replace Brandon. The team played well and reached the final, where they were up against their rivals, Glendale Primary. By half-time the score was even: 2–2. Then disaster struck. Ten minutes into the second half, Martin fell, trying to save the ball. The sports coach examined his ankle and told him to leave the field.

Then Kim had a brainwave. "Put me in!" she cried. The coach hesitated. He knew that Kim could play well as she was captain of the girls' team. He did not know if she was strong enough to play on the boys' team.

"Let her play," pleaded the boys. The coach nodded his head, and Kim took up her position in goal.

The Glendale team laughed when they saw a girl in goal, and their supporters mocked her. They changed their minds when Kim stopped ball after ball from going into goal. Nothing could get past her. In the final minutes of the match, Bel-Air scored again and the trophy was theirs. Kim had done the impossible.

1 Who played in the final of the tournament?

2 Which team last won the competition?

3 What is the meaning of the phrase 'in a class of his own'?

  a He preferred to play alone.

  b He was the only goalkeeper in his class.

  c He was more talented than all the other goalkeepers.

4 Why was Brandon unable to play in the match?

5 How do you think this made him feel?

6 A *brainwave* means

  a a headache.   **b** a good idea.   **c** a silly idea.

7 Explain in your own words the meaning of the sentence: 'Then disaster struck.'

8 How did the Glendale team feel when Kim went to keep goal? Give reasons for your answer.

Story structure

Stories must have a **beginning**, a **middle** and an **end**.

Beginning	Middle	End
Introduces the characters. Tells us what the story is about.	Tells us what the characters do and what problems they have.	Sorts out problems. Tells us how things finish, and the lesson learnt.

1 Work in pairs. Discuss the story 'A Match to Remember'.

- What happened at the beginning of the story?
- What happened in the middle?
- What happened in the end?

Language   Simple past tense

Regular verbs

> The **simple past tense** tells us about actions that were completed in the past. To make the simple past tense:
> For **regular verbs**, we add -ed or -d to the root verb
> play + ed = played   hesitate + d = hesitated

Verbs ending in a vowel + consonant: double the last letter and add -ed.
stop + ed = stopped   prefer + ed = preferred
Verbs ending in -y: change *y* to *i* and add -ed.
cry + ed = cried   try + ed = tried

1 **Copy and complete the sentences with simple past tense verbs.**
  1 The students (**practise**) for the match every day.
  2 The coach (**plan**) to put Martin in goal.
  3 The goalkeeper (**try**) to stop the ball.
  4 Kim (**hurry**) to take up her position in goal.
  5 The injured goalkeeper (**hop**) off the pitch.
  6 Everyone (**clap**) for Kim.
  7 The winning team (**carry**) the trophy back to school.
  8 The coach (**organise**) other matches with other schools.

Irregular verbs

Many verbs are **irregular** in the past tense. There is no rule for forming these verbs. You just need to know them.
know – knew: The team knew that no one could replace Brandon.
Remember: The past tense of is/are is was/were.

1 **Find the simple past tense of these verbs in the story.**
  learn   spread   choose   strike   fall   tell   have   take

2 **Match the simple present and past tenses.**
  Example: begin – began

begin come get eat find give		made sat got went began ate
get go make pay see sit		saw gave found came paid

3 **Retell the story in the simple past tense.**

needed

Before Jason's party, his Mum <u>needs</u> (1) to go shopping. She <u>takes</u> (2) a basket with her. In town she <u>sees</u> (3) some of her friends. They <u>chat</u> (4) for a while then she <u>goes</u> into the supermarket. She <u>gets</u> (5) flour and eggs for Jason's birthday cake. When she <u>arrives</u> (6) home, she <u>realises</u> (7) that there <u>is</u> (8) no sugar in the cupboard. She <u>asks</u> (9) her neighbour, Mrs. Paul, if she <u>has</u> (10) any sugar. Mrs. Paul <u>gives</u> (11) her a packet of sugar and Mum <u>bakes</u> (12) the cake.

3 Questions

We use did + the root form of the verb to ask **questions in the simple past tense.**
Did Bel-Air win the trophy?

1 Change these sentences to questions.

Example: Kim played in goal. *Did Kim play in goal?*

1 Brandon felt ill on the day of the tournament.
2 The coach chose Martin to be in goal.
3 The players on the other team laughed at Kim.
4 André lost his football boots.
5 Bel-Air scored more goals than their rivals.

For most **wh- questions in the simple past**, we use did + the root form of the verb:
Which trophy did Bel-Air win?
For some questions, we use the simple past form of the verb: Who won the trophy?
Which team scored the most goals?
Note: The verb be always uses was in the simple past tense: Was Kim a good goalkeeper?

2 Write questions.

Example: who/win/match *Who won the match?*

1 where/the students/practise
2 how many/goals/Bel-Air score
3 what/happen/in the end
4 what/the coach say/to Kim
5 why/the players/laugh at her
6 which team/play/better

We use did not + the root form of the verb
for **negative sentences in the simple past**.
Brandon did not play in the tournament.

3 Write negative sentences.

Example: André scored a goal. *André did not score a goal.*
1 The sports coach chose Kim for the team.
2 She stopped all the balls.
3 My team won the trophy this year.
4 My parents went to the match with me.
5 I thought my school team played very well.
6 Kim met her friends after the match.

Words — Sequencing

When we describe an event or retell a story, we must say what happened in the correct **sequence**. We can use sequencing words such as first, next, then, after that and in the end to help us.

Complete the passage with the sequencing words below.

next   for a few minutes   then   finally   first   at last   after

Yesterday Jason's Mum baked the cake for his birthday party. _____ (1) she mixed the butter and the sugar. _____ (2) she added the eggs and flour. She beat the mixture _____ (3) before she put it in the baking tin. _____ (4) she put the cake in the oven. Half an hour later, she took the cake out and left it to cool. _____ (5) the cake was cool enough to ice. _____ (6) she iced it, she decorated it with chocolate drops. _____ (7) the cake was ready to eat.

Writing — Write a new story ending

⭐ **TASK:** Write a new ending for the story about Jason's birthday party.

Getting ideas

When you write a story or part of a story, you need to get ideas before you start to write. It can be helpful to share ideas with another student.

1 **Listen again to the story about Jason's birthday party.**

2 **Work in pairs. Share ideas for your new story ending.**
- How did you feel when you saw your first guests arrive?
- What games did you play?
- What did you eat?
- How did you feel when everyone had to go home?

1 **Write your story ending. Check it carefully and draw a picture to illustrate it.**

Listening and Speaking

1 **Work in pairs. Discuss the questions.**
- Name two famous Caribbean sportsmen or sportswomen.
- For which sports are they famous?

2 **Listen to the sports report. Discuss the questions.**
- What did you learn about Darvin Edwards' education?
- Where did he train?
- What problems has he met?
- What are his best results?

3 **Choose a sportsperson you admire.**
- Find out as much as you can about this person.
- Copy the table and record the information you find.

Name	
Date of birth	
Education	
Achievements, e.g. records, medals	

4 **Work in groups. Each group member should present the sportsperson of his or her choice.**
- Remember to speak clearly and to look at the members of your group when you speak.
- Ask the other students to tell you one thing they liked about your presentation and one thing you could improve.

Reading

Before you read: Scan the text to find the following information.

- Where was Usain Bolt born?
- When did he win his first silver medal?
- How many Olympic gold medals has he won?

Lightning Bolt

Usain Bolt is known around the world as the fastest man ever. His speed and his achievements in athletics have won him the title of Lightning Bolt. He holds many world records for running.

Bolt was born in 1986 in a small village in Trelawny, Jamaica, where his parents ran a grocery store. As a boy, he spent his time playing football and cricket in the street with his brother. Cricket was his first love, and the young Bolt's ambition was to play cricket for his country.

By the end of primary school, Bolt was already a talented cricketer. He was also the fastest runner in his school. When he moved to secondary school in 1998, his sports teacher noticed his talent for running and encouraged him to train as a sprinter.

In 2001 at the age of fourteen, Bolt competed in the national school meet for the first time. He won the silver medal for the 200 metre race. The following year he was entered for the 200 metre race at the World Junior Championship Games. He was so nervous before the race that he put his shoes on the wrong feet. This did not matter as he won the race, and became the youngest person ever to win the gold medal.

In 2002 Bolt moved to Kingston to train. At the age of 18, he was selected to represent Jamaica at the Olympic Games in Athens in 2004. However, a leg injury prevented him from performing well.

By this time, an American sports coach had spotted the talented young runner. He offered him a place to train in the USA, but Bolt refused. He continued to train in his own country.

By 2008 Bolt was ready for the Olympic Games in Beijing. His performance there amazed the world. He returned home with three gold medals. He repeated this performance four years later in 2012 at the London Olympics, taking his total of Olympic gold medals to six.

Bolt is a popular figure around the world. His easy good nature and outstanding talent have won him many fans. When the athlete to carry the Jamaican flag at the London Olympics was selected, the choice was simple: Usain St. Leo Bolt.

Comprehension

1 Which sports did Bolt play when he was a boy?

2 How old was he when he took part in the national school meet for the first time?

3 In which competition did he win his first gold medal?

4 In how many Olympic Games has Usain Bolt taken part?

5 Where does Bolt train?

    a in Trelawny   b in the USA   c in Jamaica

6 Besides the word *fast*, list two other adjectives that could be used to describe Bolt.

7 Why do you think Bolt was chosen to carry the Jamaican flag at the London Olympics?

8 Name another famous young West Indian. In which area does this person excel?

We make **notes** to record information in a shorter way. We do not need to write in sentences when we write notes. It is helpful to use **headings**. To make notes on a person's life we can create a timeline.

Making notes

Complete the timeline for Usain Bolt.

1986	Born in Trelawny, Jamaica
1998	
2001	
2002	
2004	
2008	
2012	

Language   Pronouns

Pronouns are words which take the place of nouns.
Subject pronouns (I, you, he, she, it, we, they) go before verbs,
Bolt won a silver medal.   →   He won a silver medal.

1 **Replace the subject of each sentence with a pronoun.**
Example: <u>Bolt's fans</u> try to watch all his races.
They try to watch all his races.

1 <u>Bolt</u> broke the world 100 metre record.
2 <u>Rick and I</u> watched the race on television.
3 <u>Sheena</u> is the fastest runner in her school.
4 <u>The Olympic Games</u> take place every four years.
5 <u>The 100 metre race</u> will take place tomorrow.
6 <u>Jamaican athletes</u> did very well in the Games.

Object pronouns (me, you, him, her, it, us, them) go after verbs.
The crowds cheered Bolt.   →   The crowds cheered him.

2 **Replace the object of each sentence with a pronoun.**
1 Everyone clapped for <u>Sheena</u>.   Everyone clapped for her.
2 Bolt waved cheerfully to <u>his fans</u>.
3 We all wanted <u>Darvin Edwards</u> to win.
4 Daddy bought tickets for my <u>brother and me</u>.
5 Everyone admired <u>my sister's medal</u>.
6 The Principal awarded <u>the prizes</u>.

3 **Choose the correct pronouns for these sentences.**
1 (**She / Her**) is an excellent sprinter.
2 Did you see (**she / her**) beat the school record?
3 (**We / Us**) were thrilled when our house won.
4 The Principal congratulated (**we / us**) on our victory.
5 Everyone cheered (**he / him**) when he crossed the line.
6 My friend showed me the medal (**he / him**) had won.
7 I can't find my sneakers. Have you seen (**they / them**)?
8 I think (**they / them**) are in the changing room.

4

I or me?
Remember that the pronoun I is the **subject** of the sentence. Me is the **object**.
My sister and I went to the competition.
Daddy bought tickets for my sister and me.

4 **Complete the sentences with *I* or *me*.**

1 Debra and _____ have been selected for the race.
2 Medals were awarded to Debra and _____ .
3 This is a secret between you and _____ .
4 You and _____ must keep this a secret.
5 Mother scolded Fenton and _____ for being late.
6 Brandon and _____ will not take part in the match.

5 **Replace the words in bold with pronouns**

Shanelle was good at sports. ~~Shanelle~~ *She* always came first
in races. Everyone expected **Shanelle** to win the 100
metre race on Sports Day. **Shanelle's** parents came to
watch. **Shanelle's parents** were very proud of **Shanelle**.
The competitors lined up for the race. **The competitors** were all quite nervous.
Mr. Jones, the sports teacher, counted them, then **Mr. Jones** blew the whistle
for the race to start. My friends and I all cheered for Shanelle. **My friends and I**
hoped that **Shanelle** would win.

Words ⟩ **Word building**

Many words are made up of more than one part. They consist of:

● a root word (the main part of the word)
● groups of letters added to the root word

fastest = fast + est   talented = talent + ed *Fast* and *talent* are root words.

1 **Which is the root word in each list?**

1 trainer   training   train   trained
2 selection   select   selecting   selector
3 competed   competition   compete   competitor
4 encourage   discouragement discourage   courage

2 What are the root words? Which letters have been added?

1 winner
2 running
3 higher
4 returned

5 information
6 amazement
7 championship
8 successful

9 impossible
10 uncertain
11 disagreement
12 comfortable

> We can divide words into **syllables**. Breaking words up into syllables helps us to read and spell them.
>
> Two syllables: med / al   sprint / er
> Three syllables: pop / u / lar   tal / ent / ed
> Four syllables: com / pet / i / tion   en / cou / rage / ment
> Some words have only one syllable: fan, race, flag

3 Read out each word in the list. How many syllables does it have?

selector   athlete   race   unhappiness   result   successful   winner
track   disappointed   secret   performance   encouragement   judge
ticket   achievement

4 Copy the table. Write each word in the correct column.

One syllable	Two syllables	Three syllables	Four syllables
		sel / ect / or	

Writing   Biography

⭐ **TASK: Write a biography of a well-known sportsperson. You can write about the person you chose for the speaking activity on page 28.**

1 Find out more about this person and create a timeline.

2 Write the first draft of your biography.
Divide the information into three paragraphs.
1 Early life, e.g. family, education
2 Sporting career: main achievements
3 Why you admire this person

> Remember to describe the events in the sportsperson's life in the correct sequence.

3 Revise your first draft and write a neat copy.

Listening and Speaking

1 **Close your books. Listen to the poem.**
What does the poet say about the hen? Is she
a friendly?   **b** fierce?   **c** helpful?
What happens when you try to take her eggs?

2 **Read the poem for yourself.**

The Hen

The hen is a ferocious fowl,
She pecks you till she makes you howl.

And all the time she flaps her wings,
And says the most insulting things.

And when you try to take her eggs,
She bites large pieces from your legs.

The only safe way to get these,
Is to crawl on your hands and knees.

In the meanwhile a friend must hide,
And jump out on the other side.

And then you snatch the eggs and run,
While she pursues the other one.

The difficulty is, to find
A trusty friend who will not mind.

Lord Alfred Douglas

3 **Work in pairs. Discuss the questions.**
- Why does the poet describe the hen as a 'ferocious fowl'?
- Name three other ferocious animals.
- Why do you think the hen behaves in this way?
- What is the best way to get the hen's eggs, according to the poet?

Reading

Before you read.

- List words you could use to describe a donkey.
- Note down the things you think the poet will say about the donkey.

The Donkey

I saw a donkey
    One day old,
His head was too big
    For his neck to hold.
His legs were shaky
    And long and loose,
They rocked and staggered
    And weren't much use.
He tried to gambol
    And frisk a bit,
But he wasn't sure
    Of the trick of it.
His queer little coat
    Was soft and grey
And curled at his neck
    In a lovely way.
His face was wistful
    And left no doubt
That he felt life needed
    Some thinking out.

So he blundered round
    In venturous quest
And then lay flat
    On the ground to rest.
He looked so little
    And weak and slim
I prayed the world
    Might be good to him.

Gertrude Hinds

1 How old was the donkey?

2 The poet says that the donkey's legs 'weren't much use'. This tells us that
   a the donkey could walk quite well.
   b the donkey found walking difficult.
   c the donkey could not use its legs.

3 The words *frisk* and *gambol* mean
   a to run and jump.   b to lie down.   c to escape.

4 Why do you think the donkey needed to rest?

5 Find three pairs of rhyming words.

6 Which of these statements about the donkey are true?
   a Its neck was not very strong.
   b Its coat was curly all over.
   c It seemed to find life puzzling.

7 How do you think the poet felt about the donkey?

8 Which is your favourite part of the poem?

Features of poems
Rhyme

Poems are written in lines. In many poems, the lines rhyme with one another.

The hen is a ferocious fowl,
She pecks you till she makes you howl.

1 **Find two more pairs of rhyming words in 'The Hen'.**
Which lines rhyme in 'The Donkey'?

2 **Find a rhyming pair in each word list.**

1	stick	frisk	trick	bike	sack	neck
2	book	hoof	root	half	roof	pool
3	shout	boot	round	town	count	ground

Rhythm

Most poems also have **rhythm**. This rhythm is created by having a number of stressed syllables (**beats**) in each line.

And <u>all</u> the <u>time</u> she <u>flaps</u> her <u>wings</u>,
And <u>says</u> the <u>most</u> <u>insulting</u> <u>things</u>.

3 **Read the first eight lines of 'The Donkey'.**
Clap out the rhythm. Which lines are stressed?

4 **Work in pairs. Choose either 'The Hen' or 'The Donkey'.**
Divide the poem so that each of you recites different parts. Practise reciting the poem.

Alliteration

> **Alliteration** is when sounds which are close together are repeated.
>
> a ferocious fowl (*The Hen*)
>
> His legs were shaky
>   And long and loose (*The Donkey*)

5 **Find the alliteration in the following sentences.**
1 The greedy goat gobbled the grass.
2 The funny flying fish flew through the air.
3 The whales wallowed in the waves.
4 The curious caterpillar crawled across the leaf.

6 **Write your own alliteration for the following.**
Example: a lizard   *a lively lizard*

1 a frog   3 a butterfly   5 the wind
2 a goose   4 a monkey   6 the sun

Language Adjectives

> **Adjectives** are words which tell us more about nouns. They can be placed either before or after nouns. The donkey had a grey coat. The donkey's coat was grey.

1 **Find five adjectives in the poem 'The Donkey'.**

2 **Add adjectives to these sentences to make them sound more interesting.**
Example: The donkey stood under a tree.
The old donkey stood under a tall, shady tree.

1 The hen guarded her eggs.   4 Mum bought fruit at the market.
2 The duck swam on the pond.   5 Parrots live in the forest.
3 I saw a boat on the sea.   6 There were flowers in the garden.

5 *Comparative and superlative adjectives*

> We add -er to adjectives when we **compare two** persons, animals or things:
> A donkey is taller than a goat.
> Sometimes we need to change the spelling: big – bigger   happy – happier
> With longer adjectives, we use the word more:
> A hen is more ferocious than a chick.
> Remember the special forms: good – better   bad – worse

1 **Complete the sentences with the correct adjective forms.**
1 Hens are usually (**small**) than roosters.
2 The brown hen lays (**good**) eggs than the black hen.
3 The young donkey was (**slim**) than its mother.
4 The blue butterfly is (**attractive**) than the yellow butterfly.
5 A goose is (**noisy**) than a duck.
6 Which of the two poems did you find (**interesting**)?

> We add -est to adjectives when we compare more than two persons,
> animals or things: tall – tallest   big – biggest
> With longer adjectives, we use most: the most ferocious animal
> Remember the special forms: good – best   bad – worst

2 **Use the correct adjective forms in these sentences.**
1 The blue whale is the (**large**) sea creature.
2 Pigs are the (**greedy**) animals.
3 Which is the (**intelligent**) animal?
4 I think that dogs are the (**friendly**) animals.
5 That was the (**bad**) storm of the year.
6 Yesterday was the (**hot**) day of the week.

> **Suffixes** are groups of letters we add to root words to change their meaning.
> The following suffixes **change nouns into adjectives**.
> -y: shady   -ful: careful
> -less: careless   -ish: selfish
> -able: comfortable

Words Suffixes

1 **Add a suffix from the box above to change each noun into an adjective.**
Example: rain   rainy

wonder   child   play   agree   sleep
cheer   hope   end   fool   like   cloud

2 **Copy the words below. Underline the suffixes and learn to spell them.**

breathless   valuable   peaceful   juicy   reliable
graceful   helpless   healthy

3 **Complete each sentence with one of the words above.**
  1 The newborn donkey was _____ . It could not leave its mother.
  2 When we reached the top of the hill, we were all _____ .
  3 We picked some _____ mangoes from the tree.
  4 Kia dances well; she is very _____.
  5 It is not _____ to eat too many sweets and crisps.
  6 Mum is upset because she has lost a _____ ring.
  7 The bus always arrives on time. The driver is very _____ .
  8 It was _____ sitting in Grandma's garden.

Writing   Description

⭐ **TASK: Write a description of an animal.**

1 **GETTING IDEAS**
  • Note down what you know about this animal.
  • Think of interesting words to describe it.

2 **PLANNING**

Copy the web and make notes about the animal you chose.

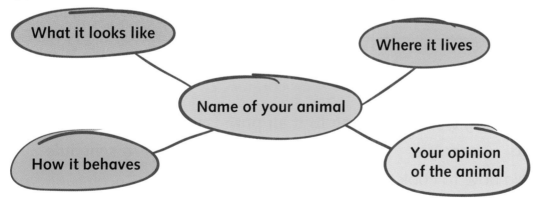

3 **Write a first draft of your description.**

4 **Revise your first draft and write a neat copy.**
Add a picture of your animal to your description.

Listening and Speaking

1 Study the information in the poster.

2 Listen to the radio announcement. What extra information does it provide?

3 Work in pairs. Prepare an announcement about an event at your school or in your community. Remember to:
- Give information about the event, e.g. time, place, price.
- Make the event sound attractive.

St. Joseph's Church

Fish Fry

Coral Beach
Saturday, 10th July
6:00 p.m.

Music from the Starlight Band

Tickets:
adults $25
children $10

Reading

There are many **different types of writing**; for example: stories, advertisements and newspaper articles. The reason for writing these pieces is known as the **purpose**. The people for whom the text is written are known as the **audience**.

Work in pairs. Discuss the questions.

1 Match the following types of writing to their purpose.

advertisements   a recipe   stories   newspaper articles   a schedule

a to tell people how to cook something
b to encourage people to buy something
c to give information
d to give the time when things happen
e to entertain people

2 **Look at the two texts on this page.**

- What types of text are they?
- For what **purpose** were they written?
- What is the **audience**?

PARTY

Lisa Joseph
requests the pleasure of

Julia James

at her tenth birthday party
Sunday, 8th March
2:00 p.m. to 6:00 p.m.

at her residence in Corinth next to Manee's Bakery

Grade 4 Trip to Pigeon Point	
Friday, 7th November	
Time	**Activity**
8:30 a.m.	Leave school, travel to Pigeon Point
9:15–11:00 a.m.	Arrive Pigeon Point, climb to Fort Rodney
11:00 a.m.–12:00 p.m.	Guided tour of museum
12:00–1:00 p.m.	Picnic on beach
1:00–2:00 p.m.	Beach cricket
2:15 p.m.	Leave Pigeon Point
3:00 p.m.	Arrive at school

Comprehension

1 Who sent the invitation?
2 How long will the event last?
3 Where will it take place?
   a in a restaurant   **b** at someone's house   **c** in the church hall
4 What kind of information should you include in an invitation?
5 Where are the Grade Four students going on their school trip?
6 What is the first thing they will do there?
7 What will they do after they have had lunch?
8 What do you think the students should take with them on this trip?

1 What is Krispy Krunch?
  a a drink   **b** a type of biscuit   **c** a breakfast cereal
2 What should you add to Krispy Krunch before you eat it?
3 What is the purpose of this advertisement?
4 What is the most likely audience?
  a children   **b** mothers   **c** teachers

Fact and opinion

A **fact** is a piece of information which is true.
Krispy Krunch contains no added sugar. – Fact
An **opinion** is something which we think is true.
Children love Krispy Krunch. – Opinion

1 **Find one more fact and one more opinion in the advertisement above.**

2 **Which of the following statements are facts? Which are opinions?**
  1 The shop sells cereals, milk and bread.
  2 The cereal is really good for you.
  3 Grandma's cakes are the best in the world.
  3 I love going to the shopping mall.
  4 The mall closes at 6:00 p.m.

Language **Future tense**

We use the **future tense** to tell us what will happen in the future. It is formed from the helping verb will + a root verb.
Grade Four will go to Pigeon Point tomorrow.

1 **Read Mum's schedule for tomorrow. Write sentences.**

Example: *She will walk to town at 9 o'clock.*

Wednesday, 12th December
9:00 a.m.   Walk to town
10:00 a.m.   Go to shopping mall
12:00 p.m.   Meet Mrs. Lewis for lunch
2:30 p.m.   Collect Jaydon from school
3:00 p.m.   Take Jaydon to dentist
6:00 p.m.   Make dinner for family
7:00 p.m.   Choir practice

2 **Answer the questions.**
1 When will you go home today?
2 What will you do after school?
3 What will you eat for breakfast tomorrow?
4 Where will you go on the weekend?

Possessive adjectives

We use the words my, your, his, her, its, our and their to tell us who owns things. They are **adjectives**. They go before nouns.
The students ate their picnic on the beach.

1 **Complete the sentences with a word from the list below.**

my   his   her   its   our   their
1 I eat _____ breakfast at 7 o'clock every day.
2 The dog wags _____ tail when it sees me.
3 My Mum and Dad eat _____ breakfast before me.
4 After breakfast my brother and I pack _____ bags.
5 Dad drives to work in _____ car.
6 My sister walks to school with _____ friends.

6

2 **Choose the correct words to complete the sentences.**

1 Every morning Mummy prepares breakfast for (**me** / **my**).
2 Greg forgot (**him** / **his**) lunch box today.
3 I gave (**him** / **his**) some of my sandwiches.
4 We waited for (**us** / **our**) parents after school.
5 The students did not listen to (**them** / **their**) teacher.
6 She was vexed with (**them** / **their**).

> **Remember:** me, him, her, it, us and them are pronouns.
> My, his, her, its, our and their are adjectives.

Possessive pronouns

> Mine, yours, his, hers, ours and theirs also tell us who owns things. They are **possessive pronouns**. They go after the verb.
> These sandwiches are mine.

3 **Complete the dialogue with the correct words.**

Greg: I forgot (**my** / **mine**) sandwiches.
Josh: Here, have one of (**my** / **mine**).
Greg: Thanks. Mmmm! (**Your** / **Yours**) sandwiches are delicious.
Teacher: Greg! Is this lunch box (**your** / **yours**)?
Greg: No, Miss. Kim has lost (**her** / **hers**) lunch box, I think this is (**her** / **hers**).
Teacher: Kim, here are (**your** / **yours**) sandwiches.
Kim: I'm not hungry, Miss. Kellie and Dana shared (**their** / **theirs**) sandwiches with me.

Words   Abbreviations

> We use **abbreviations** to write words in a shorter way. Abbreviations are often used in posters and advertisements. We put a **full stop** after an abbreviation:
> Sun. 8th Jan. (Sunday, 8th January)
> We do not put full stops after measurements:
> 100 g (100 grams), 20 km (20 kilometres)

1 **Rewrite using abbreviations.**

1 Monday, 16th September
2 Saint John's Church
3 Doctor Ernest White
4 Post Office Box
5 Beach Road
6 West Indies

2 **Read the advertisements. Find the abbreviations. Write them out in full.**

Sale   Mon. 20th–Fri. 24th Jan.   Sale

BEST BUY VEHICLES CO.

Sale   12, High St., Gros Islet
Tel: 45 3715

SPORTS CAMP

Wed. 12th Aug.–Sat. 15th Aug.

St. Mary's School, Bridge Rd.
Open to students 9–13 yrs.

$10 per session
Tel: 45 2873 for more info.

3 **Create an advertisement for your local newspaper for a yard sale at your church.**

Include the following information:

- The date and time of the sale
- Where it will take place
- Other information, e.g. contact details of organiser

When you place an advertisement in a newspaper, you have to pay for the size of the advertisement. Use abbreviations in your advertisement.

Writing

⭐ **TASK: Create a poster advertising a product.**

1 **Choose a product, for example:**

- a cheesy snack
- some sports equipment
- a new computer game

2 **Plan your poster.**

- Think of a name for your product.
- Note down the information you will include in your poster.
- Plan the layout of your poster. What pictures will you include?

3 **Make a rough draft of your poster.**

Show it to another student. Ask this student:

- Is the information in the poster clear?
- What do you like about the poster?
- What could be improved?

4 **Revise the poster. Copy it onto a clean sheet of paper.**

Before you read: Skim the letter.

- Why is Mervin writing?
- What is he writing about?

12 High Street,
New Gardens,
Saint Lucia.
12th December, 2016

Dear Ethan,

I hope you are well. Please give my best wishes to your Mum and Dad.

I am staying with my cousin Rufus in Saint Lucia. This is my first visit to the island, and my aunt and uncle have taken us to see a lot of interesting places. Yesterday we went to Morne Coubaril, which is an old sugar estate near the town of Soufrière. A guide showed us around and explained everything to us.

The first thing we saw were some huts made from bamboo. The guide told us that the Arawaks used to live in huts like these. The Arawaks were the first people to live on the island. They were hunters and fishermen.

Next we went to see the old sugar processing plant. There was a machine which crushed the sugar cane and extracted the juice. We saw a donkey working a wheel to turn the machinery.

In the past the estate also grew cocoa. The guide showed us a cocoa tree with cocoa pods on it. He cut one open for us. I was surprised to see the white pulp inside. It is hard to imagine that this pulp is used to make chocolate.

By the end of the visit we were hot and thirsty, so our guide cut the tops off some coconuts and gave us straws to drink the warm juice inside. It was really refreshing.

Before we left, we walked around the small botanical garden. I could only recognise a few of the plants, but luckily they all had labels so I knew what they were.

After we left the plantation, my aunt and uncle took us to the beach in Soufrière, where we had a picnic and swam in the sea. There was a wonderful view of Saint Lucia's famous Pitons from the beach.

I am looking forward to seeing you again when I get home. I have lots of photos to show you.

Your friend,
Mervin

Comprehension

1 Where is Morne Coubaril?
2 What were the Arawak huts made of?
3 What was used to turn the machinery in the sugar processing plant?
4 The word *extracted* means
   a removed   **b** poured   **c** stored
5 Why do you think Mervin was surprised by the white pulp in the cocoa pod?
6 What did Mervin have to drink at the end of the visit?
7 Why does Mervin use the word *luckily* when he says, "luckily they all had labels"?
8 Which other places do you think Mervin's aunt and uncle will take him to see?

Language Nouns

1 **Which nouns in the list below are proper nouns? Rewrite them using capital letters.**

cocoa   uncle kevin   micoud   guide   england   airport   january   cousin
tourist   rodney bay   supermarket bay   walk   grandmother   mrs. james

2 **For each sentence, find the noun type given in brackets.**
1 Rufus was waiting for his cousin at the airport. (**proper**)   *Rufus*
2 The crew of the aircraft was very friendly. (**collective**)
3 Mervin only had a small suitcase. (**common**)
4 When I opened the door, I had a big surprise. (**abstract**)
5 The whole family was waiting for us. (**collective**)
6 There was great excitement when we got home. (**abstract**)

Sentences

1 Which of the following are sentences? Which are phrases? What punctuation should the sentences have?

1 The drive across the island
2 Did you enjoy the visit to the plantation
3 We learned about how chocolate is made
4 A wonderful view of the Pitons
5 After we left the beach

2 Use the phrases in Exercise 1 to make sentences.

3 For each sentence, write the subject. Is it singular or plural?

1 Mervin lives in the USA.   Subject: Mervin, singular
2 Mervin's uncle and aunt took him to a lot of places.
3 The plants in the botanical garden were quite rare.
4 The old sugar mill does not work any more.
5 The Arawaks' huts were made of bamboo.

4 Copy the sentences. Underline the subject. Draw a wavy line under the predicate.

1 The students enjoyed the class visit.
2 My friends and I often go swimming.
3 I went out with my uncle in his boat.
4 The old wooden house was at the top of the hill.
5 The lizard darted across the path.

Verbs

1 Choose the correct verb forms for these sentences.

1 Mervin and his mother often (**visits** / **visit**) Saint Lucia.
2 Mervin (**loves** / **love**) visiting the island.
3 The guide (**knows** / **know**) a lot about the Arawaks.
4 Chocolate (**is** / **are**) made from cocoa beans.
5 The boys sometimes (**goes** / **go**) fishing on the weekend.

2 Find the simple past tense forms of the verbs below in Mervin's letter.

1 show showed 3 take   5 swim   7 explain   9 have
2 see   4 know   6 go   8 give

3 **Complete the sentences with the simple past tense of the verbs in brackets.**

drank
1 We (**drink**) coconut water through a straw.
2 We (**eat**) our picnic on the beach.
3 My cousin (**meet**) me at the airport.
4 Mervin (**write**) a letter to his cousin.
5 The boys (**walk**) around the botanical garden.

Adjectives

Complete the sentences with the correct adjective forms.

taller
1 Mervin is (**tall**) than his cousin.
2 I am (**big**) than my brother.
3 The (**small**) person in my family is my little sister.
4 It was (**hot**) on the beach than in the garden.
5 I think the (**beautiful**) flower of all is the rose.
6 Which was the (**interesting**) visit you made?

Pronouns

Replace the underlined words with pronouns.
1 <u>My cousin Jack</u> lives in England.   *He lives in England.*
2 I hope to visit <u>Jack</u> one day.
3 <u>My sister and I</u> love going shopping.
4 My mother often takes <u>my sister and me</u> shopping.
5 On Sundays we sometimes visit <u>my grandparents</u>.

Words   Alphabetical order

Select the word which follows next in each list.
1 baseball   basketball   cricket   _____
   a golf   **b** football   **c** athletics
2 mango   melon   orange   _____
   a plum   **b** pineapple   **c** pawpaw
3 beans   carrots   corn   _____
   a cabbage   **b** chillies   **c** dasheen
4 bat   bird   butterfly   _____
   a crab   **b** caterpillar   **c** bear

Root words

Write the root words and the letters which have been added.

Example: instruction = instruct + ion

1 smaller
2 impossible
3 discover
4 untrue

5 truthful
6 completed
7 recycle
8 invitation

9 happiness
10 government
11 helpless
12 preparation

Syllables

Divide these words into syllables. Copy the table and write them in the correct column.

Example: student   stu / dent

1 athlete
2 telephone
3 basketball
4 television

5 alphabet
6 yesterday
7 running
8 improvement

9 competitor
10 market
11 disagreement
12 understanding

Two syllables	Three syllables	Four syllables
ath / lete		

Suffixes

1 **Add suffixes to the words in the cloud to make new words.**

Example: grace + ful =   graceful

-able   -ful   -less
-ish   -ly

grace   near   child   comfort   friend   value
truth   use   respect   colour   self   love

2 **Complete each sentence with a word you made in Exercise 1.**

1 Grandma has a new bed which is very _____.
2 Share your sweets with me. Don't be _____.
3 The flowers in the Botanical Gardens are very _____.
4 Don't lose that watch. It's very _____.
5 Jason never tells lies. He is always _____.
6 Maria painted a _____ picture of her home.

Abbreviations

1 Find the abbreviations in the poster. Write them in full.

YARD SALE

St. James' Parish Hall
Harbour Street
Sat. Jan. 21, 2:00 – 4:00 p.m.
Followed by BBQ

Tickets from: D. Thompson, P.O. Box 124, Coral Bay
Tel: 442 6709

Example: *Saint James' Parish Hall*

2 Rewrite using abbreviations.

1 Thursday, 4th October
2 Doctor Jane Lewis
3 Saint Michael's Road

4 United States of America
5 Fifty dollars
6 South East

Writing Friendly letter

⭐ **TASK:** Write a letter to a friend or family member about a visit to a place of interest.

1 Plan your letter.
Include the following information.
- Where you went
- Who you went with
- What you saw and did there
- How you felt about the visit, and why

Make a list of words you could use to describe the place you visited.

2 Write the first draft of your letter. Remember to include the five parts of a friendly letter:

1 The heading
2 The greeting
3 The body
4 The closing
5 The signature

3 Check the first draft of your letter. Write a neat copy.

> ### Listening and Speaking

1 **Look at the picture. Predict what the story will be about.**
Who are the characters? What are they doing there?

2 **Listen to the story.**
Were your predictions about the story correct? What was different?

3 **Work in pairs. Summarise what happened in the story.**

4 **Discuss the questions.**

- Why did Anansi invite Turtle to share his meal?
- How did he trick Turtle?
- How do you think Turtle felt at the end of the story?
- Which other stories do you know about Anansi?

Reading

Before you read: Skim the story.
What do you think it will be about?

MONKEY AND ALLIGATOR

Once upon a time, Monkey was on a deserted island near a vast river searching for food. He had walked for hours and hours and he was exhausted. He saw a mango tree and climbed up it slowly. He could not find any fruit. "That does it!" he cried in despair. "I suppose I shall just starve to death."

"Oh no, you shall not!" cried a loud booming voice. Monkey looked down and saw Alligator.

"I saw a tree full of ripe, juicy fruits this morning on the other side of the river," Alligator said, smiling broadly.

"Really?" asked the famished monkey. He imagined the sweet delicious fruits and his mouth began to water. "How will I get to it?" he asked excitedly.

"Just climb on my back and I will take you there," Alligator replied.

Monkey knew that Alligator was cunning. He had tricked many animals before. However, Monkey was so hungry that he was willing to take the risk. He climbed down the tree and got on to Alligator's back.

"Thank you, Alligator, you saved my life," said Monkey.

Alligator grinned and said nothing. He swam upstream swishing his powerful tail from side to side. After a while, Monkey became suspicious. He could not see any sign of the tree that Alligator had spoken about.

"Alligator!" Monkey exclaimed. "Where is this mango tree?"

Alligator laughed loudly. "You silly monkey. There is no mango tree. My wife is ill. She needs some monkey's liver soup to cure her."

Monkey shook with fear. But like Alligator, he was very cunning. He immediately thought of a plan. "I wish I could help you, but I don't have my liver with me," he said. "I took it out this morning and I forgot to put it back. I left it on a tree. If you swim back there, I will get it for you."

Alligator was thrilled. He thought to himself, "How stupid can this monkey be?"

He swiftly turned around and headed for the place they had come from. As soon as Alligator reached the river bank, Monkey leapt off his back and scampered up the tree.

"Alligator, you old fool!" he called out. "Did you think that you could trick me? I have my liver right here inside me."

Alligator looked up at Monkey. He knew that he had been outwitted. He turned away slowly and crawled back into the river.

1 Why did Monkey climb the mango tree at the beginning of the story?
2 Where was Alligator?
3 Why did Alligator offer to take Monkey to the mango tree?
4 What caused Monkey to become suspicious?
5 In the sentence '"Really?" asked the famished monkey', the word *famished* means

   a very tired   **b** disappointed   **c** very hungry

6 Both characters in the story told lies. What lie did each character tell?
7 Do you think it was right for the characters to tell lies? Give reasons for your answer.
8 Which one of the animals do you think is more cunning? Give reasons for your answer.

Story Structure

In many stories, the characters face problems they have to solve.

1 **Copy the table and make notes about:**
- The problems faced by each character
- The actions they took to solve these problems
- The outcome (what happened)

Character	Problems	Actions	Outcome
Monkey			
Alligator			

Language Quotation marks

Just climb on my back.

The exact words people say are written inside **quotation marks**.
"Just climb on my back," Alligator said.

1 **Look at the story. Find four sentences with quotation marks.**

Write the words the characters said.

Example: "That does it!" he cried in despair. *That does it*

2 **Rewrite these sentences using quotation marks.**

Example: Monkey tricked me, said Alligator.

"Monkey tricked me," said Alligator.

1 There aren't any mangoes on the tree, Monkey complained.
2 Alligator called, Come down from that tree, Monkey.
3 Did you know that story? our teacher asked us.
4 I love stories about animals, Jaydon said.
5 Sheena said, I think that Alligator was very foolish.
6 I think Monkey was very brave, Kirk told me.

> We put a punctuation mark at the end of each piece of speech. It goes before the quotation mark. Sometimes we write the name of the speaker and the verb of speaking in the middle of the speech.
> "Alligator!" Monkey exclaimed. "Where is this mango tree?"

3 **Rewrite the conversation using quotation marks.**

Good evening, Anansi, said Turtle. Can I share your meal?
Hello, Turtle, said Anansi. Sit down and help yourself.
Thank you, Anansi, Turtle replied.
Turtle, your hands are dirty! shouted Anansi. You must wash them.
I am sorry, Turtle apologised. I will wash them in the river.
Don't come back until they are clean, Anansi told him.

4 **Write the dialogue as a conversation.**

Example: *"What is your favourite story?" Amy asked Kirk.*

Amy: What is your favourite story?
Kirk: I'm not sure. I like lots of stories.
Amy: I love Anansi stories. He is always so clever.
Kirk: I think Anansi is often very selfish.
Amy: That's true. The stories are very funny though.
Kirk: I prefer stories about adventures. They are more exciting.

We use a **dictionary** to find the meanings and spellings of words. Words are listed in alphabetical order. You will find the following information on each page.

Guide words: Help us to know which words are on the page
Head words: One of the words listed in the dictionary
Definition: What the word means
Example: An example of the word used in a sentence

1 **Study the extract from a dictionary page**

book   boot — Guide words

Head word — **book** [noun] set of pages fastened together which contains different forms of writing: *There are a lot of stories in this book.*

Definitions

Part of speech — **book** [verb] buy tickets or arrange to do something at a specific time: *We booked our flight to Barbados.*

Example

2 **Look in your own dictionary. Find the answers to the questions.**

1 What is the first guide word beginning with **k**?
2 What is the first head word beginning with **d**?
3 In the sentence 'Monkey cried in despair', what is the meaning of the word *despair*? What part of speech is the word *despair*?
4 How many definitions can you find for the word *trick*?

3 **Follow the example to write a dictionary entry for each word.**

Example: *foolish: (adjective) stupid or unwise*

Words	Parts of speech	Definitions
foolish	adjective	make someone feel afraid
foot	noun	part of body at end of leg
forest	verb	very angry
Friday		area of land covered by trees
frighten		stupid or unwise
furious		sixth day of the week

Writing Story

Many stories have the following elements:
Setting: When and where the story takes place
Characters: The people or animals in the story
Problem: A situation the characters must solve
Events: What happens in the story
Resolution: How the characters solve the problem at the end of the story

1 Listen to the story about Anansi and Turtle again.

2 Copy and complete the story map below about this story.

Title	Anansi and Turtle
Setting	
Characters	
Problem	
Events	
Resolution	

⭐ **TASK:** Write your own story about an animal that tricked another animal.

1 **PLANNING**

Copy the story map above. Use it to plan your story.

2 **Write the first draft of your story.**
Read it to another student. Ask this student to comment on your story.

3 **Revise your story. Use this checklist to help you.**

CHECKLIST: Have I
Told the story in the correct sequence? ❑
Included interesting words and phrases? ❑
Written in full sentences? ❑
Used correct spelling and punctuation? ❑

1 What can you see in the photograph? What would you expect to see on a walk in the forest?

2 Listen to what the guide tells the students. Discuss the questions.

- Where are the students? What are they going to do?
- Why are the forests in danger?
- What might the students see in the forest?
- What will they see in the mini-zoo?
- What instructions does the guide give them before they leave?

Reading

Before you read: Scan the text.

Which trees and animals does it mention?

Our Forests

1 There is a saying that dogs are man's best friend. However, some people prefer to say that forests are man's best friend. Forests cover most of the interior of Saint Lucia. There are many different types of trees growing in our forests, such as mahogany, gomier, red cedar and pine. Some of them, like the cedar, grow to magnificent heights.

2 Trees have many uses. They provide lumber for constructing our homes and making furniture for schools and offices. Wood can also be used to make charcoal, which provides fuel for coalpots. However, people are cutting down too many trees and destroying the forests.

3 Many beautiful and rare birds such as the Saint Lucian parrot, commonly known as the Jacquot, nest among the leaves and branches of the trees. Other animals such as the iguana, agouti and opossum also make their homes in the forest. They depend on the seeds and fruits of the trees for their food. If the trees are cut down, these creatures will have nowhere to live.

4 We cannot live without water, and trees protect our water supply. When rain falls, tree roots and branches and the dead leaves on the ground prevent the water from rushing down the hills. The water soaks into the ground instead and can be stored. Slowly it feeds the springs and the rivers which provide water for our homes, hospitals and schools.

5 Trees also provide us with the oxygen we breathe. They clean the air and absorb the carbon dioxide we breathe out. They release the oxygen our body needs. Some people say they are 'the lungs of the planet'.

6 We need trees to survive. We must all do our best to preserve our forests. When a tree is cut down, we should plant another one to replace it. In this way we will do a great service to our community and to future generations.

Comprehension

1 Name three different trees found in the forests in Saint Lucia.
2 What is lumber?
   a wood used for fuel   **b** furniture made from wood
   c wood used for building
3 Why are forests important for birds and animals?
4 What would happen to our water supply if we cut down too many trees?
5 What do our lungs do? Why are forests sometimes called 'the lungs of the planet'?
6 List three ways in which forests are important for humans.
7 What advice does the writer give about protecting forests?
8 Which of the following would be the best title for this text?
   a The Forest and Man
   b Why Forests Are Important
   c Animals of the Forest

Language   Present continuous tense

> We use the **present continuous tense** to say what is happening now.
> We add -ing to the verb and use the helping verb am, is or are.
> The guide is speaking to the students.
> The students are listening to the guide.

1 **Complete these sentences with** *am,* *is* **or** *are.*
1 We _____ walking through the rainforest.
2 I _____ looking for animals in the forest.
3 The animals _____ in the trees.
4 My friends _____ coming with me.
5 Our teacher _____ telling us about our trip.
6 It _____ getting very hot under the trees.

> For some verbs, we drop the final e before adding -ing:
> make – making: We are making charcoal.
> Some verbs double the last letter:
> cut – cutting: People are cutting down too many trees.

2 Add *-ing* to the verbs below. Make three lists.

help   dig   eat   live   take   plant   replace
drop   breathe   build   plan   put

Add -ing	Drop -e, add -ing	Double last letter, add -ing
helping		

3 Complete the paragraph with present continuous verbs.

are walking

The students (1 **walk**) along the Union Trail. A guide (2 **lead**) them. He (3 **point out**) the plants and the trees. The teacher (4 **take**) photos. Suddenly they see an agouti. It (5 r**un**) along the path in front of them. Then the guide shows the students a parrot. It (6 **sit**) on the top branch of a tree. It is hot under the trees and the students (7 **feel**) thirsty. Some of them (8 **drink**) water from their bottles. Most of them (9 **get**) tired. They (10 **look**) forward to eating lunch.

Words   Synonyms

Synonyms are words that are the same or nearly the same in meaning.
There are many magnificent trees in the forest.
There are many wonderful trees in the forest.
Magnificent and *wonderful* are synonyms.

1 **Match the synonyms.**

Example: quiet – silent

quiet
deserted   delicious
strong   rare
interesting
excellent

fascinating
tasty   superb   silent
lonely   uncommon
powerful

2 Replace the underlined words with synonyms from the list below.

end   thrilled   frightened   go   huge   flew   sad   unsafe

1 There was an <u>enormous</u> tree at the edge of the forest.
2 The students were <u>delighted</u> with their visit.
3 The tour will <u>finish</u> after visiting the mini-zoo.
4 Soon it will be time to <u>leave</u>.
5 The students were <u>sorry</u> when they left the forest.
6 It is <u>dangerous</u> to leave the trail in the rainforest.
7 Some of the students were <u>scared</u> when they saw a snake.
8 The eagle <u>soared</u> high above the trees.

Antonyms

Antonyms are words that are opposite in meaning.
The large snake slid across the path.
The tiny snake slid across the path.
Large and *tiny* are antonyms.

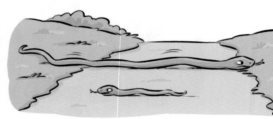

1 In each word group, choose the antonym of the word in bold.

1 **lovely:** pretty   nice   ugly   nasty
2 **plump:** small   slim   greedy   light
3 **confident:** brave   silly   sure   nervous
4 **dangerous:** safe   risky   easy   popular
5 **weak:** feeble   strong   sick   horrible

2 Replace the underlined words with antonyms from the list below.

leave   disappointed   remembered   shallow   difficult
    correct   seldom   smooth

1 Tim <u>forgot</u> to bring a bottle of water.
2 We <u>often</u> walk in the rainforest.
3 The dog had a <u>rough</u> coat.
4 The water in the pool is quite <u>deep</u>.
5 The teacher was <u>pleased</u> with the students.
6 The bus will <u>arrive</u> soon.
7 Keisha gave the <u>wrong</u> answer to the question.
8 The solution to the problem was quite <u>simple</u>.

A **paragraph** is a group of sentences about a topic. Paragraphs have a main idea which tells us what the paragraph is about. The other sentences in the paragraph give details about the main idea. Each paragraph starts on a new line.

Main idea — <u>Trees have many uses.</u> They provide lumber for constructing our homes and making furniture for schools and offices. Wood can also be used to — Details make charcoal, which provides fuel for coalpots. However, people are cutting down too many trees and are destroying the forests.

1 **Match the main ideas below to the paragraphs in the text about forests.**

- Trees help us to breathe.
- Forests are important for birds and animals.
- We must try to preserve our forests.
- Trees protect our water supply.

2 **Plan a paragraph on two of the following topics.**

- Why trees are important
- An animal that lives in Saint Lucia
- My favourite place

Copy the diagram. Use it to make notes for your paragraphs.

Main idea ← Details

3 **Write your paragraphs. Check them carefully.**

- Do your ideas make sense?
- Have you written in full sentences?
- Does each sentence start with a capital letter and end with a full stop?

Listening and Speaking

1 **Look at the picture. What can you see?**
Think of words to describe the sea.

2 **Close your books and listen to the poem. Then read it for yourself.**

Waves

There are big waves and little waves,
Green waves and blue,
Waves you can jump over,
Waves you dive through,
Waves that rise up
Like a great water wall,
Waves that swell softly
And don't break at all,
Waves that can whisper,
Waves that can roar,
And tiny waves that run at you
Running on the shore.

Eleanor Farjeon

3 **Work in pairs. Discuss the questions.**
- Name two things the poet says you can do with waves.
- What does the poet mean by 'a wall of water'?
- Find two examples of alliteration in the poem.

4 **Copy the table and enter the following details about waves from the poem.**

Colours of waves	Sounds they make	Sizes of waves	What waves do

5 **Recite the poem in pairs.**

Before you read: Look at the picture and skim the story.

Predict what it will be about.

Sea Adventure

Tyler loved the sea. His uncle was a fisherman and Tyler longed to go out fishing with him. He wanted to find out what was on the other side of the ocean that was as blue as the sky. But Tyler was only nine years old. His uncle told him that he must wait till he was thirteen before he would take him fishing.

So Tyler stayed on shore helping the fishermen as they hauled in their nets and filled their baskets with colourful fish. After a while he grew bored. He loved to see the gleaming silver fish, the small sea crabs and the speckled lobsters, but he wanted to see them swimming in the ocean, not trapped in a net.

One day Tyler decided to prove that he was old enough to go out on the sea. Like the other boys in the village, he could swim very well. He planned to do something really daring. Instead of waiting for the fishermen on the beach, he would swim out to meet them.

He waited impatiently until he saw the first canoe coming in. Then he ran quickly into the water and struck out into the sea. He planned to grab the side of the boat and jump in. He did not hear the people on the beach shouting loudly at him to come back.

Soon Tyler reached the canoe. He tried to climb aboard but the side was like a high slippery wall. He fell back into the water. He looked for the canoe but he could see nothing. The foam the canoe stirred up was like a white mist around his head. He gasped for air, but felt himself being sucked under the water. He did not know where he was.

Suddenly, Tyler felt someone pulling him out of the water. When he opened his eyes he was lying helplessly in the canoe. The fishermen looked at him angrily and one of them said, "One day you will learn".

Tyler had learnt his lesson. He would have to wait a few more years before he could go out on the ocean. For now, he would have to stay on the beach and dream of the day when he could solve the mystery of the deep blue sea.

Comprehension

1 Give two reasons why Tyler wanted to go fishing with his uncle.
2 Explain why Tyler grew bored staying on the beach.
3 What did he plan to do that was 'really daring'?
4 Why was Tyler unable to climb into the fishing boat?
5 Explain why he could see nothing when he fell back in the water.
6 Who do you think pulled Tyler out of the sea?
7 Why do you think the fishermen were angry with Tyler?
   a They did not want him in their boat.
   b He had behaved foolishly.
   c He had damaged their boat.
8 Do you think that Tyler should have been punished for what he did? Give reasons for your answer.

Features of poems

We often find similes in poems or descriptive writing. Similes compare a person, animal or thing to something else. They use the words like or as.
Examples: Waves that rise up like <u>a great water wall.</u>
The ocean that was as <u>blue as the sky.</u>

1 **Find two similes in the story 'Sea Adventure'.**

2 **Use your own ideas to complete the similes.**
   1 The water in the pool was as cold as _____ .
   2 The shark had teeth like _____.
   3 The sea was as smooth as a _____ .
   4 Tyler could swim like a _____ .
   5 The waves sounded like _____ .
   6 The scales of the fish gleamed like _____ .

Personification describes a thing as if it were a person.
Examples: Waves that can <u>whisper</u>,
Waves that can <u>roar</u>.
The poet writes about the waves as if they could whisper or roar like people.

3 **Find the personification in these sentences.**
1 The angry waves pounded the beach.
2 A gentle breeze played with the trees.
3 The warm sun kissed the flowers.
4 The wind whistled around the house.
5 The boat's engine coughed and died.

Language **Adverbs**

Adverbs tell us more about verbs. Some adverbs tell us how the action happened.
Example: Tyler waited impatiently.
We add -ly to most adjectives to form adverbs.

1 **Find four more adverbs in the story 'Sea Adventure'.**

For adjectives ending in -l, we double the *l* to make the adverb: careful – carefully
For adjectives ending in -y, we change the y to *ily*: noisy – noisily
For adjectives ending in -le, we drop the e: gentle – gently
Note the special form: good – better

2 **Change these adjectives to adverbs.**

quiet   greedy   cheerful   sensible   busy   grateful

3 **Use the adverbs you made in the sentences below.**
1 Tyler waved _____ to his uncle from the shore.
2 The birds pecked _____ at the fish.
3 Tyler thanked the fisherman _____ for rescuing him.
4 He listened _____ to what the fisherman told him.
5 The fishermen worked _____ mending their nets.
6 I think that Tyler did not behave _____ .

Some adverbs tell us where, when or how often the action happened.
Where: "The fishing boats are here!" shouted Tyler.
When: I went fishing yesterday.
How often: Tyler went to the beach every day.

4 **Find the adverbs. Copy the table and write them in the correct column.**
1 We will go fishing tomorrow.
2 The fisherman keep their boats outside.
3 It rained all night.
4 My older brother often goes fishing.
5 We looked everywhere for the missing dog.
6 The market takes place monthly.
7 I could not see any of my friends there.
8 Next year I will be old enough to go fishing.

Where	When	How often
	tomorrow	

Comparative and superlative adverbs

Comparative adverbs compare two actions.
Tyler swam faster than the other boys.
For some adverbs, we add -er to compare: harder, faster, earlier
For most adverbs ending in -ly, we add the word *more*: more quickly
Note the special forms: well – better   badly – worse

1 **Complete the sentences with comparative adverbs.**
1 The boats arrived (**soon**) than we expected.
2 The market opened (**late**) than usual.
3 My teacher told me to speak (**slow**).
4 The weather was much (**bad**) in the evening.
5 The fisherman told Tyler to behave (**responsible**).
6 He told him to think (**careful**) before going in the water.

Superlative adverbs compare more than two actions.
Example: Tyler swam the fastest of all the boys in the village.
For some adverbs. we add -est to compare: hardest, earliest, fastest, latest
For most adverbs ending in -ly, we add *most*: most quickly
Note the special forms: well – best   badly – worst

2 Complete the sentences with superlative adverbs.
1 Kia was the (**early**) to arrive at the beach party.
2 Ben was the (**late**) to arrive.
3 Kayla behave the (**sensible**) at the party.
4 Ben and Tim shouted the (**noisy**).
5 Greg ran the (**slow**) of all the boys.
6 We all thought that Kayla danced the (**good**).

Writing   ## Description

⭐ **TASK: Write a description of one of the following places. It can be a place you know or an imaginary place.**
       a a beach   **b** a waterfall   **c** a forest

1 Copy the web. Make notes about the place you chose.

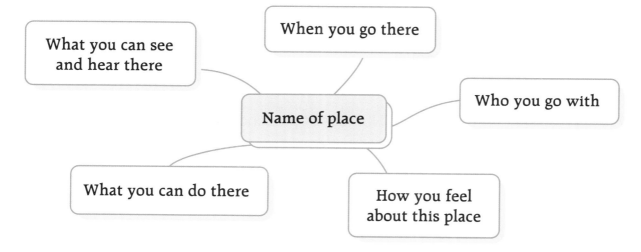

2 Write a first draft of your description.
Remember to use interesting words. Try to include some similes.

3 Revise your first draft and write a neat copy.

Listening and Speaking

1 **The picture shows some things which were invented in the past 150 years.**
Which one do you think has made the biggest difference to our lives?

2 **The students in Brandon's class were asked to choose an important invention and give a presentation about it.**
Listen to Brandon's presentation.

> Before you listen: look carefully at the headings in the table below. They will tell you what you need to find out.

3 **Copy the table and make notes.**

The Aeroplane	
Name of inventors	
Date of first flight	
Date of first flight across Atlantic	
Length of journey	
Modern passenger planes	Number of passengers: Time in air: Speed: Height:

4 **Work in pairs. Discuss the questions,**
- What three inventions do you think have made the biggest difference to people's lives?
- What difference have they made?

Reading

Before you read: Think of as many different reasons as you can why people use computers.

www.kidsfacts.schools.com.computers   search

Science Facts for Kids

| Animals | Plants | Environment | Human | Body | Technology |

History of the Computer

Most people think that the computer was invented in the 20th century. This is not quite true. People have used the abacus, which is a simple form of computer, for thousands of years. In 1832, **Charles Babbage**, a British inventor, started work on the world's first mechanical computer. He planned to make a machine that could work out sums and print out the results. The machine was so complicated that Mr. Babbage was never able to finish it.

The very first modern computer was made in **Manchester University**, England in 1948. This machine was so huge that it filled a whole room. It was the first machine which had a memory which could store information.

Computers today

Nowadays, computers come in different sizes. Some are so small that they fit on your lap and can be carried easily from one place to another. Today many people have tablet computers or smartphones which they can use when they are on the go.

Computers are useful in many ways. People can use them at work or in their free time. We can keep in contact with friends and family who live a long way away by sending emails or calling them on **Skype**.

Computers make learning fun for children. They can use the **Internet** to find out information for their school projects. There are computer games which help them with subjects like Mathematics or Spelling. They can also have fun playing games or listening to music on-line.

One important use for computers is in factories. Have you ever heard about **robots**? They are machines that can do many kinds of jobs that people do. Computers control robots, telling them what to do. Robots often do difficult and dangerous tasks such as welding, cutting and drilling.

Computers are also used in hospitals. Doctors use them to find out what is wrong with patients. Some special **X-ray machines** use computers to give a picture of the inside of the body. Computers also help nurses to monitor their patients and find out when they need help.

Computers have made a big difference to the lives of disabled people. Some computers can 'speak' and so they are used to read books to the blind. Other computers have been designed to control wheelchairs so that disabled people can move about.

Comprehension

1 What was the world's first simple computer?

2 Why is Charles Babbage important?

3 What was the main difference between the first modern computer and the computers we have today?

4 To use something 'on the go' means

  a to use something all the time.

  b to use something when you are away from home.

  c to use something at home or in the office.

6 In what ways can children make use of computers?

7 Are the following statements true or false?

  a Robots are machines that can replace people at work.

  b It is not safe for robots to do welding or drilling.

  c X-ray machines tell nurses when patients need help.

  d Blind people can use computers to listen to books.

8 Name two other groups of people who use computers at work.

Features of a website

> A **website** is a collection of pages on the Internet.
> At the top of the website you will find the **URL** (the address of the website).
> You will also find a list of the different **web pages** on the site.
> Websites often include **hyperlinks**. If you click on a hyperlink, it will take you to another website which has useful information on the topic.

1 What is the URL for the 'Science Facts for Kids' website?

2 How many web pages are there on this site? What topics are they about?

3 Find three hyperlinks in the website.

Language **Conjunctions**

> **Conjunctions** are words we use to join sentences.
> You can send emails to your friends. You can call them on Skype.
> You can send emails to your friends and you can call them on Skype.
> The new sentence has only one capital letter for 'you', and one full stop.

1 **Match the sentences. Join them with *and*.**

1 Children can use computers for research.   They can control wheelchairs.

2 You can play games on-line.   They can weld it together.

3 Computers can read books to blind people.   They can play computer games.

4 Computers can cut metal.   You can listen to music.

> We use the conjunction and to add extra information. We use but to show contrast.
> I switched the computer on but it did not work.
> We use so to show result.   I did not know the answer so I looked it up on the Internet.

2 **Complete the sentences with *and*, *but* or *so*.**

1 I would love to have a new computer _____ I do not have enough money.

2 I am saving money _____ I can buy a new computer.

3 My friend sent me an email _____ I did not receive it.

4 My sister can send texts from her phone _____ she can take photos.

5 Our old computer did not work _____ we bought a new one.

6 My brother has a new tablet _____ he uses it for his work.

3 **Use your own ideas to complete the sentences.**

    1 We can use computers to do calculations and _____.

    2 I would like to have a smartphone but _____.

    3 We go to the computer room once a week so _____.

> We use the conjunction because to give a reason.
> Computers are useful because you can use them for research.
> We use although to add unexpected or different information.
> Many students have cell phones although they may not use them at school.

4 **Join the sentences with *although* or *because*.**

    Example: *We should learn to use computers because they help us with our work.*

We should learn to use computers.		They help us with our work.
Grandpa has a computer.		He does not use it often.
Mum sent her friend a text.	although	She was going to be late.
I sent my cousin an email.		I wanted to give her my news.
I often take pictures on my phone.	because	They are not very good.
Most children love computer games.		Some of them play for too long.
Ben is not able to use a computer.		He is too young.

Words   **Suffixes**

> The following **suffixes** change words into nouns.   -ion: instruction
> -ation: information   -ment: arrangement   -dom: freedom   -y: difficulty

1 **Add a suffix from the box above to change each word into a noun.**

You may need to change the spelling of the word. Use your dictionary to help you.

Example: *invent – invention*

invent   **wise**   **arrange**   **introduce**
product   **examine**   **advertise**   **honest**

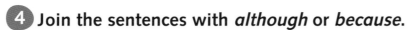

2 **Copy the words below. Underline the suffixes. Learn to spell the words.**

decision   argument   permission   revision   donation   amazement

3 **Complete each sentence with one of the words from the list above.**

1 Kim and her sister had an _____ about the new computer.
2 My uncle gave me _____ to send a text on his smartphone.
3 Thanks to a generous _____, the school bought some new computers.
4 Kirk gasped in _____ when he saw his brother's new camera.
5 Tara made notes to help her with her _____ for the examination.
6 The Principal took the _____ to ban students from using phones at school.

Writing

⭐ **TASK: Write a report about ONE of the following inventions.**

- The motor car
- The telephone
- Television

1 **Find out more about the invention you chose,**

Write questions to guide your research. Use the following question words.

What?   When?   Where?   Who?   Why?   How?

Make notes about your research.

2 **Divide your information into sections.**

Example:
- Name of inventor and when and where it was invented
- How the invention is used
- Why it is important

3 **Write the first draft of your report.**
Write one paragraph for each section.

4 **Revise your first draft and write a neat copy.**

Listening and Speaking

1 **Look at the picture. What do you think is happening?**

2 **Work in pairs. Discuss the questions.**
- What problem did Jaydon have?
- What did he decide to do about it?
- Do you think he did the right thing?

3 **Give your opinion of the story.**
- Did you find the story interesting? Why?
- Which part of the story did you like best?
- Is there any part of the story that you did not like? Give reasons for your answer.

Reading

Before you read: Skim the story.
Who is the main character? What problem did she have?

Computer Brain

Computer Brain
You cause me pain
Just like a light
You are so bright.
Switch you on
The sum is done.
Computer Brain
You'll go insane.

These were the first words Kellie heard every time she entered the schoolyard. At first she hid her head and hurried towards her classroom. But now it didn't matter any more. Kellie walked past with her head held high.

It all started when Kellie wanted a bicycle. She first learned to ride on her friend's bike. After falling off many times, she was finally able to balance and ride around the block. One day she saw the bike of her dreams in a store. It cost $500.

Kellie went home and checked the amount of money in her piggy bank. There were four twenty-five cent pieces, eleven fifty cent pieces, four five dollar notes and two ten dollar notes.

"How much more money do I need?" Kellie thought to herself. She worked out the sum on a piece of paper. "$453.50!" she exclaimed. "How will I ever make that sum of money?" She thought for a moment. "I know. I will do odd jobs after school and on Saturdays."

Kellie explained to her parents what she wanted to do. "We will help you buy the bicycle," her father said, "but you must not get behind at school."

Kellie was excited. "I promise I will work hard," she said. The next day she put her plan into action. She started by washing the neighbours' cars and weeding their gardens. At the end of the week, she checked the money she had been paid and worked out how much she still had to save.

Every week, Kellie did odd jobs, and every week she checked how much she needed to save. She was always adding, subtracting, multiplying and dividing. She became very quick at working out the sums. After a while she was able to do them in her head.

Soon Kellie began to do well in Mathematics lessons. When her teacher asked a question, Kellie's hand always went up first. She always had the answer. While the other students were struggling to solve problems with pen and paper, Kellie worked them out in her head.

Her classmates grew jealous. They teased her and nicknamed her 'Computer Brain'. Kellie was upset at first, but then she took no notice. Before long she had collected $250. Her father agreed to give her the rest of the money she needed.

Now Kellie is the proud owner of a shiny new bike. She whizzes past the other children on her way to school. She does not hear them shouting, 'Computer Brain'. Her mind is on other things. She is thinking of how to save up for a computer.

Comprehension

1 Why did the other students call Kellie 'Computer Brain'?
2 What odd jobs did Kellie do?
3 Give two more examples of odd jobs that children can do.
4 Kellie's father said he would help her if she did not 'get behind' at school. To *get behind* means

   a to be bottom of the class.

   b to do badly in your school work.

   c to sit at the back of the class.

5 Where did Kellie keep the money she saved?
6 Explain why Kellie started to do well in Mathematics lessons.
7 How much money did Kellie's father give her?
8 What lesson do we learn from this story?

Cause and effect

The **cause** is why something happens. The **effect** is what happens.

Cause	Effect
The students were jealous of Kellie.	They teased her.

1 Identify cause and effect in these sentences.
1 Kellie was upset. The students teased her.
3 Kellie started saving money. She wanted to buy a bicycle.
4 Kellie has saved enough money. She has bought a bicycle.
5 Kellie's parents are proud of her. She is doing well at school.

2 **What will be the effect of these actions?**

1 James worked hard learning his spellings.

2 The students made a mess in their classroom.

3 Shanice twisted her ankle on the way to the match.

3 **What do you think caused these situations?**

1 Chantelle was late for school.

2 Our team lost the match.

3 Brad's parents were proud of him.

Language **Possessive nouns**

We use an **apostrophe** with s to show that something belongs to someone.
Kellie's new bike
When the noun is **plural** or ends with s, we put the apostrophe after the s.
The students' books   Mr. Jones' computer
Note the special forms: the children's toys   the women's children
the people's choice

1 **Rewrite using apostrophes.**

Example: the bike which belongs to Kellie   *Kellie's bike*

1 the bags which belong to the students

2 the computer which belongs to my mother

3 the things which belong to the men

4 the house which belongs to Mr. Charles

5 the office which belongs to the Principal

6 the computer game which belongs to Lucas

2 **Take words from each column and write sentences. Remember to add apostrophes.**

Example: *Kayla's uniform was very neat.*

1	Kayla	school
2	the boys	uniform
3	the children	bedroom
4	my friends	car
5	Mrs. Davis	shoes
6	the twins	clothes

Prefixes are groups of letters we place in front of root words to change their meaning. The prefixes un-, dis- and mis- mean *not*.
Examples: happy – unhappy   honest – dishonest
understand – misunderstand

1 **Join the prefixes to the words in the cloud to give them the opposite meaning.**

Example: *unhelpful*

un-   dis-
mis-

helpful
agree   cover
behave   approve   place
sure   obey

2 **Choose words from Exercise 1 to complete the sentences.**

You may need to change the words to make them fit the sentences.

1 Mr. Samuel was vexed because the students _____ the rules.
2 He told the students not to _____ when he left the room.
3 Kellie _____ that her bike had a puncture.
4 Kirk was _____ of the answer to the question.
5 Grandma has _____ her glasses.
6 Josh was _____ when I asked him how to do the problem.
7 My friend thinks the story is interesting but I _____ .
8 Anna _____ of the way the other students teased Kellie.

The prefix re- means *again*.
To reread means to *read again*.

3 **Add the prefix *re-* to the verbs below.**

play   plant   cycle   build   place   write

4 **Complete the sentences with the verbs you made in Exercise 3.**
1 My teacher told me to _____ the exercise neatly.
2 I helped Grandpa _____ the broken window.
3 The students _____ the trees in the school yard.
4 We can _____ the paper we use in class.
5 The teams will _____ the match on Saturday.
6 After the storm we had to _____ our house.

5 Choose two words for each prefix (*un-*, *dis-*, *mis-*, *re-*). Write them in your own sentences.

Letter of thanks

⭐ **TASK: You are saving up to buy something you really want like a bicycle or a computer. Your aunt has given you some money. Write a letter to thank her.**
Include the following information:
- What you want to buy and why
- What you are doing to save money

1 **PLANNING**
Make notes for your letter.
<u>What I want to buy:</u> new bike
<u>Why:</u> old bike too small
<u>How I am saving money:</u> help in neighbour's garden

2 **DRAFTING**
Write the first draft of your letter.
- Start by thanking your aunt.
- Use the layout for a friendly letter from page 15.

3 **REVISING**
Check that you have included all the required information.
Make sure that your sentences make sense.
Write a neat copy of your letter.

4 **PROOFREADING**
Proofread your letter. Use this checklist to help you.

CHECKLIST: Have I
Started each sentence with a capital letter? ☐
Put a full stop or a question mark at the end? ☐
Used commas in the address? ☐
Spelled tricky words correctly? ☐

Listening and Speaking

1 **Discuss in groups: Do you think students should wear uniforms to school?**

2 **Listen to the conversation between Mark and Jessica.**

3 **Work in pairs. Discuss the questions.**
- Give two reasons why Jessica does not want to wear school uniform.
- What does Mark say to Jessica about uniforms?
- Which student do you agree with? Why?

4 **Work in groups. Prepare for a debate on the following topic:**

Students should wear uniforms to school.

One half of the group writes points in favour of wearing uniforms to school. The other half of the group writes points against wearing uniforms.

Ask your teacher to organise a class debate on the topic.

Reading

Look at the letter on the next page. Identify the features of a formal letter.

A **formal letter** has the same features as a friendly letter:
1 the heading **2** the greeting **3** the body **4** the closing **5** the signature
In addition, above the greeting, it should have **the name and address of the person to whom you are writing**.

Randville Post Office,
Randville,
Saint Lucia.
10th November, 2016

Mrs. Mathurin,
The Principal,
Randville Primary School,
Randville,
Saint Lucia.

Dear Mrs. Mathurin,

I am writing on behalf of the students of Grade Four to request a Dress Down Day for the school. We think it would be a good idea to hold this event on National Colours Day on 22nd February. Instead of wearing their uniforms, students could dress in the colours of the national flag.

We suggest that our school can use this day as a fundraising day. Each student who dresses in the national colours can pay a minimum contribution of $1.00. They can pay more if they wish. We can also ask our parents to prepare some snacks to be sold at break time. The money raised in this way can be used to purchase more reading books for our library. This will help students to become better readers.

We believe that a Dress Down Day will benefit both the students and the school. The students will feel more relaxed since they will not have to wear their uniforms. The day will also help to show off their creativity in designing the clothes they wear.

If this day is successful, we think that the school could organise a Dress Down Day once a term to raise funds. We hope that you will consider our suggestion.

We are looking forward to a response from you.

Yours sincerely,
Jessica Johnson
Grade Four Student

Comprehension

1 Who is the letter from?
2 What is the purpose of the letter?
3 What does 'a minimum contribution of $1.00' mean?
 a Students may not pay more than one dollar.
 b Students can pay more than one dollar.
 c Students can pay less than one dollar.
4 On which day will students dress down?
5 What will the money they raise be used for?
6 Which other way of raising money does the writer suggest?
7 Summarise the ways in which the Dress Down Day will benefit students.
8 How would you raise funds to benefit students in your school?

Language Formal and informal language

We use formal language when we speak to people in authority and when we write. We use informal language to speak to our friends and family.

Hey Mark! How are you doing?

Good morning, Mrs. Mathurin.

1 Find examples of formal language in the letter on page 83.

Example: *I am writing on behalf of the students of Grade Four.*

2 Read the sentences below. Do they contain formal or informal language?
1 Children should wear uniform to school.
2 Wearing uniform's not cool.
3 Thank you for allowing us to have a Dress Down Day.
4 Thanks. That's great.
5 Wow! I love your dress.
6 Can you tell me where you bought your new shirt?

Punctuation

We use commas in letters:
- after each line of the address and between the month and the year.
- after the greeting and the closing.

We put a full stop at the end of the last line of the address.

1 Study the punctuation in the letter on page 83.

2 Write the following addresses and dates correctly.

> Bellevue,
> Beach Street,
> Sandy Bay,
> Grenada.
> 2nd May, 2017

1 Sunnyview Primary School Long Road Newtown 5th January 2016
2 P.O. Box 268 Vieux Fort Saint Lucia 14th December 2016
3 Palm Beach Hotel English Harbour Antigua West Indies 1st June 2017
4 The Manager Thompson's Bakery High Street Rodney Bay 10th March 2017

We also use commas to separate items in a list.
The colours of the Saint Lucian flag are yellow, white, blue and black.
We do not usually put a comma before *and*.

3 Rewrite the sentences below using commas.
1 We study Maths English Social Studies and Science at school.
2 My uniform consists of a white shirt blue trousers black socks and black shoes.
3 I packed my books my pen my dictionary and my lunch box in my bag.
4 The tuck shop sells juice biscuits sweets and crisps.

4 Use your own ideas to complete the sentences.
1 My favourite sports are _____ .
2 I like to eat _____ for lunch.
3 The names of my friends at school are _____ .

> Write at least three items in each list.

12 Conditional sentences

> A conditional sentence is a sentence where one action depends on another.
> If we raise money, we will buy books for the library.
> In the 'if' part of the sentence, we use the **present tense**. In the other part of the sentence, we use the **future tense**.

1 Match the sentences in the table.

Example: *If everyone pays $1.00, we will raise a lot of money.*

1 If everyone pays $1.00
2 If our parents prepare snacks
3 We will wear the national colours
4 If the Principal agrees
5 If the Dress Down Day is successful
6 We will feel more relaxed
7 We will become better readers

a if we have a Dress Down Day.
b if we wear our own clothes.
c if we have more books.
d we will sell them at break time.
e we will have a Dress Down Day.
f we will raise a lot of money.
g we will do it again next term.

2 Use your own ideas to complete the sentences.

1 If I have enough time, I will _____ .
2 If I get up early, I will _____ .
3 If I ask my mother, she will _____ .
4 If I have enough money, I will _____ .

 Words   Homophones

> Homophones are words that sound alike but have different spellings and meanings.
> Wear: Students can wear their own clothes on Dress Down Day.
> Where: I do not know where I put my uniform

1 Complete each sentence with the correct homophone.

1 The students were (**aloud** / **allowed**) to wear their own clothes.
2 The teacher wanted to (**sea** / **see**) me after the lesson.
3 The Principal received a (**check** / **cheque**) for $500 for the library.
4 Xavier put his shoes on the wrong (**feat** / **feet**).
5 There was a book (**sale** / **sail**) at the end of term.
6 Please help me to (**sew** / **sow**) the button on my shirt.

2 **Match the words in the list to the definitions below.**

sail   sale   root   route   pair   pear

1   part of plant which is under the ground
2   a type of fruit
3   to travel somewhere by ship
4   a set of two things of the same type
5   event where people buy and sell things
6   road you use to go somewhere

Writing   **Formal letter**

⭐ **TASK: Write a letter to your school principal requesting that she asks the cook to change the lunch menu.**

1 **GETTING IDEAS**

Work in pairs. Discuss the following questions.
● Why do you want the menu to be changed?
● What types of food would you like to have on the lunch menu?
● What will be the effect of changing the menu? How will you feel?

2 **PLANNING**

Plan the body of your letter. Use the ideas from your discussion.

3 **Write the first draft of your letter.**

Write one paragraph for each section.

4 **Revise your first draft. Use the checklist below to help you.**

CHECKLIST: Have I

Included the six elements of a formal letter?   ☐
Explained the reasons for writing the letter?   ☐
Used formal language?   ☐
Written in sentences and paragraphs?   ☐
Punctuated the letter correctly?   ☐

Reading

Before you read: Survey the text below.

What kind of text is it?

What do you think it will be about?

The King's Watchman

Once there lived a king who had a large amount of money. He was afraid that someone would steal it, so he employed a watchman to guard it day and night. After some years, the watchman took ill and died. The king had to find someone to replace him.

"People have become greedy nowadays," the king thought to himself. "Where will I find someone as honest as my faithful old servant?"

After many sleepless nights, the king came up with a plan. He sent his servants all over the country to tell people that he was looking for someone to guard his money. Anyone interested in taking the job was invited to a banquet at the palace in a fortnight's time.

The night before the banquet, the king ordered his servants to spread coins over the floors of the rooms leading to the banqueting hall. The servants were puzzled, but they did as he commanded. Soon the floors were covered with gold and silver coins. Never before had anyone seen so much money.

The next morning, the gates of the palace were opened and dozens of men were let in. On their way to the banqueting hall, they passed through room after room where the floors were covered in coins. Strangely, there were no guards in sight.

The king was waiting for them beside a table laden with all sorts of delicious foods. He greeted them and invited them to sit down and eat their fill. After they had eaten, the king made an announcement.

"Before I choose my new watchman, I would like to see all of you dance. I will give the job to the man who dances best," he said.

The band started playing, and a skinny old man with a white beard jumped up and began to dance. He danced and danced and never seemed to grow tired. The other men sat there and watched. They did not get up.

The king laughed to himself. His plan had worked. He knew that the others did not dare to get up and dance as their pockets were full of the coins they had stolen on the way to the banqueting hall. The old man was the only honest man among them. The king was happy for him to become his new watchman.

Comprehension

1 Why did the king need a watchman?
2 Why do you think the king had sleepless nights?
3 What is a banquet?
4 Why were the king's servants puzzled?
5 What did the men who came for the watchman's job see on the way to the banqueting hall?
6 Why does the writer use the word *strangely* in the sentence 'Strangely, there were no guards in sight'?
7 How do you think the men felt when the king asked them to dance?
   a tired   **b** afraid   **c** greedy
8 What lesson do we learn from this story?

Copy and complete the story map.

Title	The King's Watchman
Setting	
Characters	
Problem	
Events	
Resolution	

Language Punctuation

Rewrite the sentences below using quotation marks.

Example: Will you be my watchman? the king asked.

"Will you be my watchman?" the king asked.

1 The king wants a new watchman, the messenger announced.

2 I need money, said one man. I want the job.

3 The king declared, You all tried to cheat me.

4 Who is that old man? everyone asked.

5 I trust you, said the king. You can be my watchman.

6 The old man replied, I will never try to cheat you.

Verbs

1 **Add *-ing* to the root verbs in the list below.**

look   dance   laugh   stop   make   plan   clap   sit   try   run

Example: *look – looking*

2 **Complete the sentences with present continuous verbs.**

is dancing

1 The old man (**dance**) to the music.

2 The other men (**watch**) him.

3 I (**write**) a story about a king.

4 The students (**take**) books out of the library.

5 It (**get**) late now.

6 We (**wait**) for our friends.

Conjunctions

Use *and*, *but* or *so* to make two sentences into one sentence.

Example: *The old man saw the money but he did not take it.*

The old man saw the money.		He did not take it.
The king played a trick.	and	He could see who was honest.
The others saw the money.		They put it in their pockets.
The old man heard the music.	but	He got up to dance.
The old man was honest.	so	The king chose him.
I enjoyed the story.		I did not like the ending.

Possessive nouns

Rewrite using apostrophes.

Example: the king + watchman   *the king's watchman*

1 the teacher + desk
2 the children + books
3 Mrs. Charles + son
4 my grandparents + house
5 my brothers + toys

Adverbs

1 Form adverbs from the adjectives in the list below.

honest   quiet   happy   helpful   good   proud   greedy   thankful

Example: honest   *honestly*

2 Which adverbs would you use to describe how you do the following actions?

1 listen to your teacher   *quietly*
2 run to catch a bus
3 shout to someone who is a long way away
4 use a knife to cut a mango
5 wait for a friend who is late

Words   Prefixes

1 Add prefixes to the words in the cloud to make new words.

Example: un + kind = *unkind*

| un-   re- |
| dis-   mis- |

cover   kind   pay   treat   agree   fortunate
honest   place   like   cycle   sure   understand

2 Complete each sentence with a word you made in Exercise 1.

1 Kim is upset because her friend was _____ to her .
2 The _____ student did not tell the truth to her teacher.
3 I must _____ the money that I owe you.
4 We can _____ a lot of the things we throw away.
5 We should look after animals. We should not _____ them.
6 I _____ people who show off all the time.

Synonyms

1 **Write a synonym for each word below.**

1 unhappy *sad*	**4** feeble	**7** brief
2 large	**5** powerful	**8** quiet
3 begin	**6** courageous	**9** remain

2 **Rewrite each sentence replacing the underlined word with a synonym.**

1 These flowers are <u>pretty.</u>

2 I was very <u>glad</u> to meet them.

3 The new student is extremely <u>clever.</u>

4 The cut on my finger is very <u>sore</u>.

5 It is <u>unsafe</u> to swim out to sea.

6 The <u>enormous</u> giant chased Jack down the road.

7 Mum was <u>angry</u> when she saw Amy's untidy bedroom.

8 Grandma provided some <u>delicious</u> snacks for the party.

Antonyms

Complete the sentences with antonyms of the underlined words.

1 Your glass is <u>empty</u>. Let me give you a <u>full</u> one.

2 Do not go into <u>deep</u> water. Stay where it is _____.

3 The <u>narrow</u> lane leads to a _____ road.

4 I <u>forgot</u> my shopping list today. I must _____ it tomorrow.

5 The children were <u>asleep</u>, but Grandpa was _____.

6 The <u>tiny</u> boy ran after the _____ dog.

Homophones

Choose the correct homophones to complete the sentences.

1 _____ are my socks? I need to _____ them to school. (**wear / where**)

2 I need a new _____ for my boat. I will buy one in the _____. (**sale / sail**)

3 James could _____ untie the _____ in his shoelaces. (**knot / not**)

4 The _____ was painted a _____ blue. (**plain / plane**)

5 Keira _____ her new bike down the _____. (**road / rode**)

6 Does the shop _____ computer games? (**cell / sell**)

7 The _____ school was painted during the holidays. (**hole / whole**)

Study skills Dictionary

Match the words and the definitions. Write a dictionary entry for each word.

Example: *crab (noun): creature with shell and claws*

Words	Parts of speech	Definitions
crab	adjective	make something new
crawl	noun	bright red in colour
create	verb	young animal, e.g. bear, lion
crimson		cloth which covers a window
cub		make a sick person better
cure		creature with shell and claws
curious		move slowly, move like a crab
curtain		wanting to find out about something

Writing Story

⭐ **TASK: Write a story with the title 'Honesty is the Best Policy'.**

1 Plan your story. Use these questions to help you.
- Who is the main character in your story?
- Is this character honest or dishonest?
- What did he or she do?
- What will happen at the end of your story?

2 Complete a story map about your story.

3 Write the first draft of your story.
Try to include some conversation.

4 Revise your story. Use the checklist on page 57 to help you.

Unit 13

Listening and Speaking

1 **Look at the photo.**

Where is it located?
What would you find there?
Why do you think it is a
protected area?

2 **Listen to Forest Officer Charles tell you about the Maria Islands.**
- Where are the Maria Islands?
- Explain what is meant by a protected wildlife area.
- Why are the Maria Islands a protected wildlife area?
- In what ways are the racer snake and the whiptail lizard similar?
- In what ways are they different?

3 **Work in pairs. Copy and complete the table.**

Name	Physical features	Habitat	Diet
Whiptail lizard	small, blue, black and yellow		
Racer snake			

4 **Choose two other animals. Complete an information table about them like
the one above.**

Reading

> **What is a reptile?**
> Reptiles are animals that are cold-blooded. This means their body temperature changes depending on where they are. They bask in the sun to keep their body heat up. Most reptiles lay eggs, and their skin is covered with hard, dry scales.

Before you read: Copy the table.

Write two things you know about reptiles and two things you want to know.

Reptiles in Saint Lucia		
What I **K**NOW	What I **W**ANT to know	What I **L**EARNT

Reptiles in Saint Lucia

Many species of reptiles are found in Saint Lucia. These include lizards and snakes. Some of these reptiles are endemic to Saint Lucia. That means they are not found anywhere else in the world.

LIZARDS

Saint Lucia iguana

The iguana is Saint Lucia's largest lizard. It can grow up to one and a half metres long. It lives in trees but you can often see it on the ground. It is green in colour with black markings. It has a long row of spines on its back. It feeds mainly on leaves but also eats flowers and soft fruits.

Saint Lucia tree lizard or zandoli

You can see the tree lizard in your yards on leaves and trees. It is able to change its colour to blend with its surroundings. This is known as 'camouflage'. In this way, it is well protected from its enemies. Tree lizards feed on insects they catch on the ground.

Saint Lucia whiptail or zando

The whiptail is a small ground lizard. Its tail is like a whip. It carries the colours of the flag of Saint Lucia: it has a blue chin and tail, its underside is bright yellow and its throat is black. It feeds on insects, flowers and fruits and small sea creatures.

SNAKES

Saint Lucia fer-de-lance or sepan

The fer-de-lance is a large snake found in rainforest areas. It has poisonous fangs which fold up in its mouth. It feeds on birds and small mammals such as rats and agoutis. The female gives birth to 30 to 40 live young at once.

Saint Lucia boa or tet chyenn

The boa is Saint Lucia's biggest snake. It can grow up to two metres in length. It is found in forests and even in banana plantations. It is harmless to humans and feeds on birds, other reptiles and small mammals. Females can give birth to more than 20 young.

Saint Lucia racer or kouwes

The racer is the world's rarest snake. It is found only on the Maria Islands. There are only around 20 racers on the islands. It feeds mainly on lizards and their eggs, and on frogs and birds. The females lay their eggs in an underground burrow.

Comprehension

1 Name four reptiles found in Saint Lucia. Give their English and Creole names.
2 How do reptiles keep their body heat up?
3 What does the term *camouflage* mean?
4 Which lizard has three different colours?
   a the green iguana   **b** the tree lizard   **c** the whiptail
5 Which lizards eat insects?
6 Which two reptiles do not lay eggs?
7 State one thing which is similar about the fer-de-lance and the boa.
8 Add two facts you learned about reptiles to the table you prepared before reading.

A, an and the are **articles**.
We use the before nouns for particular people, animals, places or things.
We use a or an before singular nouns for general things and people.
Singular nouns: The racer is a snake. It is the rarest snake in the world.
Plural nouns: The snakes on the Maria Islands are rare.

Note: We do not put an article before plural nouns for general people and things: Snakes are reptiles.

1 **Complete the sentences with articles (*a, an, the*) where they are needed.**

1 _____ whiptail is _____ lizard. Lizards are _____ reptiles.

2 _____ iguana is _____ biggest lizard in Saint Lucia.

3 You can see _____ lizards in _____ nature reserve on _____ Maria Islands.

4 _____ boa feeds on _____ birds and _____ small mammals.

5 I could see _____ egg in _____ racer snake's burrow.

6 _____ Forest Officer told _____ students about _____ work he does.

7 _____ baby snakes were in _____ underground burrow.

8 _____ iguana lives in _____ trees but you can often see it on _____ ground.

We use some when we do not give an exact quantity.
I saw some lizards in my yard.
We use any in questions and negative sentences.
Can you see any frogs in the pond? No, I can't see any frogs.

2 **Complete the dialogue with *some* or *any*.**

Kim: Did you see _____ animals on the islands?

Brad: Yes, I saw _____ birds, but I didn't see any reptiles.

Kim: Did you take _____ photos?

Brad: No, I didn't, but my uncle took _____ photos of our family on the beach.

Kim: I'd like to see _____ of his pictures. Do you have _____ of them with you?

Brad: No, but I can ask him to send you _____ .

Study the table of contents. Answer the questions.

1 On which page does the section about wildlife begin?

2 How many sections are there in the book?

3 In which section would you find the answer to the following questions?

a Which animals are endangered?

b Where can we visit old forts?

c What activities does the Trust provide for young people?

d When was the Saint Lucia National Trust founded?

e Where can I find out about visiting the Maria Islands?

Index

Study the index. Answer the questions.

1 On which pages would you find information about the following?

    a where frogs live   **c** animals living only in Saint Lucia

    b birds' nests   **d** species which could become extinct

2 Where can you find information about camouflage?

3 What kind of information can you find about butterflies?

4 What does the word *nocturnal* mean? Name one animal which is nocturnal.

Writing   Expository report

⭐ **TASK: Write a three-paragraph report about *either* an alligator *or* a turtle.**

You will need to research some facts for your report. Use an encyclopaedia or the Internet. If you use an encyclopaedia, the table of contents and the index will help you find information. If you use the Internet, type the name of the animal you chose in the search engine and you will find lots of articles.

1 GETTING INFORMATION

- First write down what you already know about the reptile.
- Next decide what you need to find out. Write this as questions.
- Make notes about the information you find.

2 PLANNING

- Write a heading for each paragraph, e.g. What the animal looks like.
- Organise the information you found under each heading.

Example:

Paragraph 1: What the alligator looks like	Grey-green colour, scaly
Paragraph 2: What it eats	

3 DRAFTING

Write your notes out in full sentences.

4 REVISING

Remember these rules:

- Write a heading for each paragraph.
- Include at least three details in each paragraph.
- Start each paragraph on a new line.

Listening and Speaking

1 **Discuss the fireman's questions.**

What happens when you have a fire drill at school?

Why is it important to have fire drills at schools?

Who do you call if a building catches fire?

What will you do if there is a fire at your school?

2 **Listen to the fireman's instructions, then work in pairs.**
Are the following statements true or false?
- When you hear the fire alarm, leave the classroom at once.
- Listen carefully to what your teacher tells you.
- Put your things in your school bag.
- Run quickly to the assembly area.
- Do not go back into the classroom without permission from your teacher.

3 **What should you do if there is a hurricane?**
Give three instructions.

Before you read: Scan the text.

What kind of text is it? What information do you expect to find?

FIRE SAFETY

Every October the Saint Lucia Fire Service observes Fire Prevention Week. During this time, the service reminds Saint Lucians to take fire safety seriously to prevent fires from breaking out.

Fire is useful in many ways. We use it to cook food. In cold countries, people use fire to keep warm. Fire is also used in many industries. However, fire can also be harmful. A fire can cause bad burns, destroy buildings and kill people and animals. In some countries, like the United States of America, fires sometimes destroy large forests. In 1948 a fire destroyed the entire city of Castries.

Fires are often started by accident. One of the most common causes of fires at home is children playing with matches. Another common cause of fires is carelessness. Everyone needs to understand the importance of fire safety. Here are some safety rules we should follow to prevent accidents with fire in our homes.

Rules for children

· Do not play with matches or candles.
· Do not poke things into electrical sockets.
· Never play near the stove.
· Check with an adult first if you want to cook something.
· Never hang clothes over light bulbs and electrical equipment.

Rules for adults

· Store matches and candles in a place where children cannot reach them.
· Put out oil lamps and candles before you go to bed.
· Keep a fire extinguisher or fire safety blanket in your kitchen.
· Never leave a fire unattended or in the care of children.
· Do not plug too many devices such as irons and kettles into wall sockets.
· Never let rubbish pile up around your home. This can be a good place for fires to start.

Comprehension

1 State two ways in which fire is useful.
2 State two ways in which fire is harmful.
3 What happened in Castries in 1948?
4 What often causes fires in people's homes?
5 Are the following statements true or false?
　　a It is a good idea to dry wet clothes over a light bulb.
　　b Children must ask for permission before they start cooking.
　　c You can let children keep watch over a fire if it is in a safe place.
　　d Fires sometimes start in rubbish piles.
6 **What is a fire extinguisher?**
　　a a device that starts fires　　b a device that puts out fires
　　c a hose used by firemen
7 Name three other devices that can be plugged into wall sockets.
8 Would you like to be a fireman? Why or why not?

Language　Instructions

We use **imperative verbs** to give instructions.
Check with an adult if you want to cook something. Do not play by the stove.
Check and *Do not play* are imperative verbs.

1 **Find four more instructions in the leaflet about fire safety.**

2 **Choose the correct verbs to complete the instructions.**
Some of the instructions should be negative (*Do not*).

allow　listen　plug　keep　leave　call

1 _____ carefully to the fireman's instructions.
2 _____ children to play near a fire.
3 _____ matches in a safe place.
4 _____ piles of rubbish around your home.
5 _____ the Fire Service if you see a house on fire.

3 **Write four instructions for a fire drill at school.**
Example: *Stop what you are doing at once.*

Indefinite pronouns

We use **indefinite pronouns** to refer to people or things without saying exactly who or what they are. The following words are indefinite pronouns.

somebody	anybody	nobody	everybody
someone	anyone	no one	everyone
something	anything	nothing	everything

We use a singular verb after an indefinite pronoun.
Everyone needs to understand the importance of fire safety.

1 **Choose the correct pronouns to complete the sentences.**
  1 Please listen to the instructions, (**anyone** / **everyone**).
  2 Take (**anything** / **nothing**) with you when you leave.
  3 Did you leave (**anything** / **nothing**) in the classroom?
  4 There's (**somebody** / **anybody**) standing at the door.
  5 (**Somebody** / **Nobody**) should talk during a fire drill.
  6 There was (**anything** / **nothing**) left on the table.

2 **Complete the sentences with the correct verb forms.**
  1 Everyone (**is** / **are**) afraid of fire.
  2 No one (**wants** / **want**) to have a fire.
  3 We (**has** / **have**) a fire drill every term.
  4 Someone (**is** / **are**) still in the building.
  5 Firemen (**trains** / **train**) for a long time.
  6 Everybody (**knows** / **know**) you should not play with matches.

Negative words

Words such as no, none, not, never, nothing, nowhere and nobody are **negative** words. We should not use these words with other negative words. Combining two negatives in a sentence is an error called a **double negative**.

This is wrong: negative   negative
If there is a fire drill, you should not take nothing with you.

We should say instead:
If there is a fire drill, you should not take anything with you.

14 **1** **Choose a word from the list below to complete each sentence.**

no   nowhere   nothing   nobody   not   none

1 I checked the classroom. There was _____ there.
2 There were _____ students left in the building.
3 Keisha did _____ listen to the instructions.
4 _____ of the students were injured in the fire.
5 There was so much smoke, I could see _____.
6 I got in the bus but there was _____ to sit down.

2 **Find and correct the sentences which have double negatives.**

Example: I could not see him nowhere.   *I could not see him anywhere.*
1 Joshua did not know nothing about the fire.
2 There wasn't anyone left in the building.
3 I did not know none of the people standing outside the building.
4 We have not never had a fire in our school.
5 There were no firemen at the blaze.
6 I did not have no phone to make a call about the fire.

> Words   **Homographs**

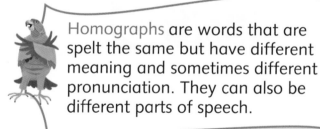

Homographs are words that are spelt the same but have different meaning and sometimes different pronunciation. They can also be different parts of speech.

Put the match back in the box.

1 **What parts of speech are the homographs in these sentences?**

1 Put another <u>stick</u> on the fire.   noun
2 Dad tried to <u>stick</u> the broken pieces together.
3 <u>Duck</u> your head when you go into the cave.
4 It was here that I saw the <u>duck</u> swimming.
5 I thought I heard the bell <u>ring</u>.
6 The teacher told the students to stand in a <u>ring</u>.

Your shoes do not match.

2 **Give another meaning for each homograph below.**

You can use your dictionary to help you.

1 sign

    A: a board with information   B: _to write your name_

2 sink

    A: submerge under water   B: _____

3 rock

    A: to move from side to side   B: _____

4 stamp

    A: a small sticker on a letter   B: _____

5 train

    A: a form of transport   B: _____

6 draw

    A: a game ending in a tie   B: _____

Writing **Instructions**

⭐ **TASK: Write a set of instructions about what to do in the case of fire.**

1 **Read the paragraph below.**

What to do in the case of fire

If you see a house on fire, you should not go inside. You must call the Fire Service and give them the address of the house. If you do not have a phone, you could ask an adult to make the call.

If you are inside a house when it catches fire, you must leave as quickly as you can. If there is a lot of smoke, it is better to crawl, as smoke rises. When you leave the house, you should close the door behind you. You should never go back into a burning house.

2 **Write a set of instructions.**

Example: _Do not go inside a house that is on fire._

3 **Use the instructions to make a notice for your classroom noticeboard.**

Use illustrations and different colours to add impact to your poster.

Listening and Speaking

1 **Look at the picture.**

What is happening? How do you think the fire started?

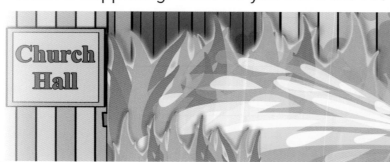

Church Hall

2 **Listen to the news report about the fire.**

3 **Work in pairs. Discuss the questions.**
- Where and when did the fire break out?
- Was anyone hurt? Who?
- What two possible reasons are given for the fire?

4 **Imagine that you saw the fire. Describe it to another student.**

Reading

Before you read: Skim the story.
- Who is the main character?
- What does he do?

Bamboo Bursting

The older boys made it look so easy. Pour kerosene into a long piece of bamboo, set light to a torch, then put the burning torch into the opening. Blow and wait for the sound, 'Booom!' The explosions echoed through the entire neighbourhood.

Greg had heard these sounds after he had gone to bed every night since mid-November. He peered out of his bedroom window and watched the boys enviously. He longed to join them, but his parents said he was too young to take part in bamboo bursting.

School was closed so Greg had time on his hands. He decided to take no notice of his mother's warning about playing with fire. One day when his parents had gone out, he went searching for bamboo. He was lucky enough to find a piece the boys had left behind under a pile of stones.

Greg took the bamboo from its hiding place and carried it home. He found the kerosene his mother had stored for emergencies and poured it into two bottles. He copied what he had seen the boys doing, but he did not get a 'Boom!'. He only got a feeble 'Pop!'.

Greg became impatient and poured more kerosene into the bamboo. He blew hard and this time there was an enormous 'Boooom!'. Greg jumped up and down in excitement. He knocked over the kerosene and it caught fire. To his horror, the flames started to spread over the floor.

Greg stamped on the flames to put them out, but it was no use. He tried throwing a towel over them, but that did not work either. He dashed to and from the kitchen sink throwing cupfuls of water on the fire. All the time the blaze kept on growing.

Soon Greg was choking in the thick smoke from burning plastic. He dashed out of the house screaming, 'Help! Fire! Help! Fire!'. The neighbours quickly formed a bucket brigade and helped to extinguish the blaze.

When Greg's parents arrived home, they found a dejected Greg sitting outside the house, sobbing his heart out.

"Why are you crying?" his father asked. "What has happened?"

"I have done something silly," Greg confessed. In sad voice, he told his parents his tale.

"Are you all right?" his mother asked anxiously. "Have you hurt yourself?"

"What damage have you done?" his father asked. He went inside to inspect the kitchen.

Now it is April, and the kitchen has been repaired. Greg's pocket money goes towards the 'Kitchen Fire Fund'. He has promised his parents never to play with fire again, and he has explained to his friends why his sneakers have charred tongues.

Comprehension

1. 'The older boys made it look easy.' What did they make look easy?
2. How did Greg feel when he watched the older boys?
   a scared   **b** jealous   **c** excited
3. Greg had 'time on his hands'. This means that
   a he did not have any free time.   **b** he did not use his time well.
   c he did not have anything to do.
4. Where did Greg find the piece of bamboo?
5. What caused the fire in the kitchen?
6. How did Greg try to put it out?
7. What explanation do you think Greg gives when he is asked about his sneakers?
8. Do you agree with the punishment Greg received? Give reasons for your answer.

Character

When we talk about a person's character, we describe the qualities that make up his or her personality.

1 **Discuss in pairs.**
- Which of the following adjectives describe Greg's character?
  sensible   obedient   thoughtless   honest   disobedient   impatient
- Give reasons for your choice.
Example: impatient – He gets impatient when the bamboo does not go 'Boom!'.

2 **Choose adjectives to describe another character in a story you have read. Explain why you chose these adjectives.**

Language **Present perfect tense**

The **present perfect tense** tells us about something which happened in the past. It does *not* tell us *when* it happened. It is formed from the helping verb has or have + past participle.

"I have done something silly," said Greg.

| helping verb | | past participle |

1 Find two more examples of the present perfect tense in the story.

2 Complete the sentences with *have* or *has*.

1 Greg's father _____ repaired the kitchen.
2 The other students _____ asked Greg about his sneakers.
3 Greg _____ not played with fire again.
4 He _____ apologised to his parents.
5 They _____ forgiven him.
6 Now his grandmother _____ bought him a new pair of sneakers.

To make the past participle, we add -ed or -d to the verb:
happen – happened   promise – promised
There are a lot of irregular past participles which you must know, e.g. do – done.

3 Match the verbs with their past participles.

Example: *be – been*

be begin break choose	chosen taken gone begun
eat find give go hide	seen broken eaten been
see speak take	hidden found spoken given

4 Complete the dialogue with verbs in the present perfect tense.

Grandma: <u>Have</u> you <u>helped</u> (**help**) your father fix the kitchen?
Greg: Yes, I _____ _____ (**wash**) the walls and Daddy _____ _____ (**paint**) them.
Grandma: What else _____ _____ you _____ _____ (**do**)?
Greg: We _____ _____ (**begin**) to mend the chairs.
Grandma: Very good. Grandpa _____ _____ (**give**) me some money to buy you new sneakers. After we _____ _____ (**eat**), we will go shopping.

15 Relative pronouns

We can join different parts of sentences with who, which or where.
The caretaker spoke to the boys who were bursting bamboo.
Greg picked up the piece of bamboo which he found under the stones.
Have you seen the building where the fire broke out?

1 **Complete the sentences with *who, which* or *where*.**
1 The caretaker ran after the boys, _____ hid in the bushes.
2 Greg looked in the cupboard _____ the kerosene was kept.
3 Greg took the can of kerosene _____ was in the cupboard.
4 Daddy repaired the chairs _____ had been damaged.
5 The reporter spoke to the fireman _____ was injured.
6 An ambulance took the fireman to hospital _____ he was treated for burns.

2 **Use your own ideas to complete the sentences.**
1 Do you know the boy who _____?
2 No one knows the cause of the fire which _____ .
3 We visited the place where _____ .

Words   Context

Look for clues to help you understand new words. You can find clues in the **context** (the words and sentences around these words).
They found a dejected Greg, sobbing his heart out.
Dejected means *sad*. The clue is in the rest of the sentence (Greg is crying).

What do the underlined words mean? Use the context to help you.
1 He did not get a 'Boom!'. He only got a <u>feeble</u> 'Pop!'.
   a loud   **b** weak   **c** frightening
2 Greg <u>peered</u> out of his bedroom window and watched the boys.
   a looked   **b** leant   **c** climbed
3 The explosions echoed through the <u>entire</u> neighbourhood.
   a large   **b** whole   **c** distant
4 The neighbours brought buckets of water to <u>extinguish</u> the fire.
   a light   **b** increase   **c** put out

Writing | Picture story

⭐ **TASK: Look at the pictures. Write a story with the title 'Mum's Birthday'.**

1

2

3

4

1 PLANNING

Complete a story plan for your story.

Title	Mum's Birthday
Characters	
Setting	
Problem	
Resolution	

2 Write the first draft of your story.

Include some conversation in your story.

3 Revise your story and write a neat copy.

Use some interesting words and phrases to make your story exciting.

Listening and Speaking

1 **Look at the photograph.**
What problem does it show? What might the result be?

Hello, kids. I'm Tin Tin and I have an important message for you.

2 **Listen to the announcement from Tin Tin.**
What message do you think Tin Tin has for children?

3 **Work in pairs. Discuss the questions.**
What happens when people throw garbage in the streets?
What advice does Tin Tin give to children?
In what other ways can we keep our environment clean?

4 **Make a list of the kinds of things people throw away.**

Example: plastic bottles

 • Which of these things rot away?
 • Which ones do not rot away?

Keep your answers and check them when you do the reading exercise.

Listen to and discuss an announcement about waste.

Reading

Before you read: Skim the text below.

- What is it about?
- What kind of information do the table below and the pie chart on the next page provide?

Every day people throw away things they do not need any more: paper, glass, plastic. Did you know that some of this waste can take hundreds of years to decay? The plastic bags and bottles people left lying around yesterday will still be there a hundred years from now for your great-grandchildren to find.

Each month, the population of Saint Lucia produces 5,500 tons of garbage. Our island is too small to house this mountain of waste. We have to find a way of dealing with it. The best way is to follow the **3R's**: **R**educe, **R**euse, **R**ecycle. We must **reduce** the amount of garbage we produce, **reuse** things instead of throwing them away and **recycle** things we cannot reuse.

How can we follow the 3 R's? We can reduce the amount of paper we use by writing on both sides. When we go shopping, we can use our own bags instead of the plastic bags supplied by the supermarket. We can reuse an empty ice-cream container by storing our lunch in it. Glass jars can be used for storage. We can send the items we cannot reuse to be recycled. In that way we can help to make a difference for our environment, our country and the world.

How long the items we throw away take to decay	
Items	Rate of decomposition
Banana peel	3-4 weeks
Newspaper	6 weeks
Apple core	2 months
Sheet of paper	2-5 months
Orange peel	6 months
Juice box	5 years
Candy wrapper	20 years
Plastic bottle	Up to 1,000 years
Potato chips bag	Up to 1,000 years
Plastic bag	Up to 1,000 years
Glass bottle	1 million years

16 The pie chart shows the garbage collected at the end of the school day in Grade Four at the Belle Plain Primary School.

Comprehension

1 The term *waste* refers to
  a unwanted items that we throw away.
  b items that can be reused or recycled.
  c items that take a long time to decay.
2 Why is it important to reduce the amount of waste produced in Saint Lucia?
3 Name one way in which you could reduce the amount of waste you produce.
4 What could you store in a glass jar?
5 Which items take hundreds of years to decay?
6 Name two items which decay quickly.
7 What was the biggest percentage of items collected in Grade Four at Belle Plain School?
8 How could the Grade Four students reduce the amount of waste they produce?

Language   Colons

We use a **colon** at the end of a sentence to introduce a list. We place a comma between each item in the list. A comma is **not** generally used before and.
People throw away things they do not need: paper, glass, fruit peels and plastic.

Answer comprehension questions. / Colons

1 **Rewrite these sentences using colons and commas.**

1 We can recycle many items plastic bottles glass jars cans and paper.
2 The Grade Four students create a lot of waste juice boxes candy wrappers pencil shavings and fruit peels.
3 There are a lot of things in the Lost Property Office books lunch boxes sports clothes and school bags.
4 Mum checked the items on her shopping list bread potatoes eggs and sugar.

2 **Complete these sentences with lists of at least four items. Remember to use colons and commas.**

1 These are the things we collected on our beach clean-up _____.
2 Don't forget these items when you pack your school bag _____.
3 We study a lot of different subjects at school _____ .

Prepositions

> **Prepositions** relate one part of a sentence to another.
> Tin Tin spoke to the students.
> Many prepositions tell you where people and things are.
> There was a lot of garbage on the ground.

1 **Find 8 more prepositions in the following paragraph.**

We all listened to Tin Tin. He said we should put our trash in the bin and not leave it around the school yard. If we go to the supermarket, we should take a shopping bag with us. We should never throw juice boxes through the bus window. When we are at the beach, we should not hide our trash under some stones. There are garbage bins on most beaches.

2 **Complete the sentences with prepositions from the list below.**

with   into   under   around   on   past

1 The lazy girl dropped her drink can _____ the ground.
2 She walked _____ the garbage bin.
3 She did not put the can _____ the bin.
4 I went to the beach _____ my friends.
5 We walked all _____ the beach picking up garbage.
6 We found a pile of garbage _____ the trees.

Some prepositions are used with expressions of time.
We had a beach clean-up on Sunday. It began at 10 o'clock.

3 **Add prepositions of time from the list below to the sentences**

before   in   after   at   during   on

1 There will be a beach clean-up _____ 1st May.
2 The beach clean-up will start _____ one hour's time.
3 The teacher gave the students instructions _____ they started.
4 The students worked hard _____ the clean-up.
5 They finished _____ midday.
6 _____ they finished, they all went swimming.

Sometimes verbs are followed by prepositions which give them a
special meaning: find + out = to discover or to learn about something
The students found out about waste.

4 **Complete the sentences with the prepositions *back*, *down* or *out*.**

1 Don't forget to give _____ the books you borrowed.
2 Our teacher handed _____ the leaflets about recycling.
3 The students got _____ to work quickly.
4 We turned _____ when we reached the end of the beach.
5 Mum pointed _____ the pile of garbage in the corner.
6 She was angry but she soon calmed _____ .

Words   Compound nouns

We can sometimes put two nouns together to make **compound nouns.**
news + paper = newspaper   class + room = classroom

1 **Match the nouns in the ovals to make compound nouns.**

black
photo   play   time
book   foot   sea
thunder

ground
board   storm   side
print   graph   case
table

2 Use the clues to find the compound nouns.

1 Your father's mother   *grandmother*
2 A person who protects you when you go swimming
3 Used to tie your shoes
4 A pain in the head
5 Work you do at home like cleaning and cooking
6 It starts life as a caterpillar

3 Choose four compound nouns from Exercise 1 or 2. Write them in your own sentences.

Writing **Write about a graph**

⭐ **TASK: Summarise the information in a graph.**

1 Study the information in the bar graph below.

It shows the number of students who took part in a beach clean-up.

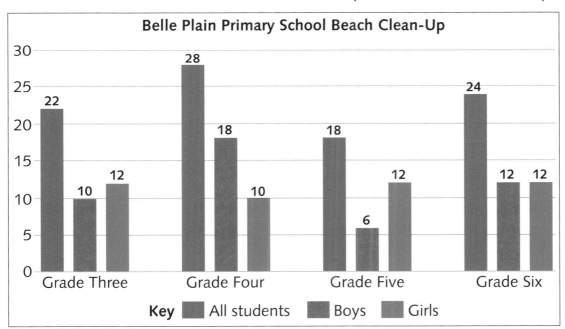

2 Work in pairs. Discuss the graph.

Examples: Ten boys in Grade Three took part in the beach clean-up.
More Grade Four students took part than students in the other grades.

3 Write six sentences about the information in the graph.

4 What do you think the students found on the beach? Write a list.

Listening and Speaking

1 **Look at the picture. Discuss the questions.**
- What are the men doing? Why do you think they are doing this?
- Is it a good idea to take sand from a beach? Why? Why not?

2 **Listen to the extract from the radio call-in programme.**

3 **Work in pairs. Discuss the questions.**
- Why is Mr. James calling the radio station?
- What reason does he give for people taking sand from the beaches?
- What is the effect of sand mining?
- Why does Mr. James think this practice should be stopped?

4 **Think of another practice which harms our environment, e.g. dumping waste. Role play a call to a local radio station about this practice.**
- Describe the practice.
- Explain why it is harmful.
- Suggest how it could be stopped.

Reading

Before you read: Survey the text on the next page.
- What kind of text is it? How do you know that?
- What is the main idea of the text?
- Which practices does it describe?

Our Homeland

Regardless of where we roam
This beautiful island is our home.
God blessed this speck of earth,
Hoping we would appreciate its worth.
In the depths of our own home ground
The sweet sounds of nature are all around.
But the clanging sound of our cutlasses,
Brings massive trees crashing to their knees.
The swooping of shovels, filling our trucks and vans,
Clears our beaches of their sparkling sands.
The dumping of garbage in our silvery streams
Poisons our rivers and pollutes the sea.
We are hurting this nature isle,
Stripping her of her lovely smile.
Let us halt our actions,
Save Fair Helen for future generations.

Williamson Beharry

Read a poem.

1 To what does the title of the poem 'Our Homeland' refer?
2 Which three ways of harming our homeland are described in the poem?
3 Give two examples of the 'sweet sounds of nature'.
4 Who do you think the poet refers to as 'the future generations'?
5 What figure of speech is the line 'Stripping her of her lovely smile'?
   a simile   **b** personification   **c** alliteration
6 How do you think the poet feels about the island where he lives?
   Give reasons for your answer.
7 What do you think was the poet's purpose in writing this poem?
8 How do you think we can we save this island for future generations?

Features of poems

1 **Find examples of alliteration in the poem.**

Example: *the swooping of shovels*

The sound of some words matches their meaning.
The clanging sound of cutlasses.
The word *clang* suggests the sound of a cutlass. Using words this way
is known as **onomatopoeia**.

2 **Match the sound words in the list below with the descriptions.**

splash   hiss   pop   buzz   whack   crash   growl   chirp

1 young birds in their nest   *chirp*
2 a tall tree falling
3 someone jumping into a river
4 bees around a hive
5 a fierce dog
6 a snake attacking its prey
7 a balloon bursting
8 a cricketer hitting a ball

3 **Write six sentences which include onomatopoeia.**

Example: *I heard the young birds chirping in their nest.*

Language Past continuous tense

We use the **past continuous tense** to say what was happening at a certain time.
We add -ing to the verb and use the helping verb was or were.
The men were taking the sand.

1 **Complete the sentences with *was* or *were*.**

1 The turtle _____ burying its eggs under the sand.
2 The people taking the sand _____ destroying the eggs.
3 The tourists _____ watching the turtles on the beach.
4 The garbage _____ poisoning the water in the river.
5 The men _____ using cutlasses to chop down trees.
6 My friends and I _____ helping to clean the beach.

2 **Answer the questions using the past continuous tense.**

Example: What was the man doing?   (**build a house**)
He was building a house.

1 What were the men doing?   (**cut down trees**)
2 What was the iguana doing?   (**lay its eggs**)
4 What were the birds doing?   (**make nests in the trees**)
3 What were the builders doing? (**take sand from the beach**)
5 What was the garbage doing?   (**block the drains**)
6 What was the policeman doing? (**stop people from sand mining**)

We often use the **simple past** and the **past continuous** in the same sentence.
When I saw the men, they were shovelling sand.

    simple past   past continous

The simple past is used for completed actions. The past continuous is used for
actions which have not been completed.

3 **Read the paragraph. Find five verbs in the simple past and five in the past continuous.**

When I was walking along the beach, I saw a group of tourists. Some of them
were lying in the sun. Some of them were swimming. A little boy was sitting
beside his mother. Suddenly, he got up and ran down to the sea. His mother
called him but he did not come back. His father went to fetch him. He scolded
him for running away. Soon the little boy was crying.

4 **Complete the sentences.**

The verbs should be in the simple past or past continuous.

saw   *was cutting down*

1 I (**see**) a man who (**cut down**) a tree.
2 The policeman (**stop**) the man who (**take**) sand.
3 When Marie (**walk**) along the beach, she (**spot**) an iguana.
4 Tim (**injure**) his foot when he (**play**) on the beach.
5 It (**rain**) when I (**go**) out.
6 While I (**wait**) for my friends, I (**hear**) a strange noise.

Words   **Using a thesaurus**

A **thesaurus** is a book which contains lists of **synonyms** (words which have a similar meaning). You can use a thesaurus to find more interesting words for your stories and poems. Today many people use an **online thesaurus**.

1 **Study these extracts from a thesaurus.**

afraid (adj.) alarmed, anxious, frightened, horrified, nervous, scared, worried

angry (adj.) annoyed, bad-tempered, cross, furious, irritated, raging, vexed

2 **Use synonyms to replace *afraid* and *angry* in the sentences below.**
1 The policeman was <u>angry</u> when he saw people taking sand.
2 I felt <u>afraid</u> when I saw the massive tree fall.
3 My mother was <u>angry</u> with me because I came home late.
4 I always feel <u>angry</u> if my friends keep me waiting.
5 Josh always feels <u>afraid</u> if he has tests at school.
6 We were all <u>afraid</u> when we saw the huge snake.

3 **Find synonyms for the words *nice* and *nasty*. Use them to make word webs.**

horrible

nice   *nasty*

pleasant

4 **Find synonyms for the words *nice* and *nasty* in the sentences below.**

1 We had a <u>nice</u> time at the beach yesterday.

2 The garbage in the river made a <u>nasty</u> smell.

3 Mum told Lisa not to be <u>nasty</u> to her little sister.

4 There is a <u>nice</u> view of the island from the top of the hill.

5 Our teacher is always very <u>nice</u> to us.

6 Tim has a <u>nasty</u> cut on his foot.

Writing   **Poem**

⭐ **TASK:** Write an acrostic about a Saint Lucian animal or bird.

1 **Study the acrostic poem.**

An **acrostic** is a poem where the first letter of each line makes up a word.

Iguanas in Danger

In our sheltered bays and coves

Green iguanas hide their eggs

Under deep layers of sand,

Away from our prying eyes,

Never suspecting that unkind men

Are coming to destroy them

Stealing sand from our beautiful beaches.

2 **Choose an animal and write your own acrostic. Try to include alliteration or onomatopoeia.**

Discuss your acrostic with another student. Ask this student to suggest how it could be improved.

3 **Write a neat copy of your acrostic on a separate sheet of paper.**

Draw some pictures to illustrate it.

Unit 18 The Last Laugh

Listening and Speaking

1 **Do you know any traditional stories or myths? When and where are they set?**

2 **Look at the picture. What do you think the story you are about to hear will be about?**

3 **Listen to the story, then work in pairs.**

Put the events in the correct sequence.
- Finally Jablotin won a game.
- Ti Jean went home to fetch his own cards.
- Jablotin invited Ti Jean to play cards.
- Ti Jean ran away and Jablotin could not find him.
- Jablotin threatened to pinch off Ti Jean's arm.
- Ti Jean won all the games and Jablotin was furious.

4 **Discuss these questions.**
- What do you think of each of the characters: Ti Jean and Jablotin?
- What do you think will happen next in the story?
- Has anyone tried to cheat you while playing a game? Retell your experience to another student.

5 **Work in pairs. Act out the scene between Ti Jean and Jablotin.**
- Think about how your character will move and speak.
- Perform your scene to another student pair. Ask them to comment on your work.

Reading

Before you read: Scan the text below.

- Who are the different characters in the play?
- How many scenes are there?

Scene 1: Beside the forest

Jablotin: Hey, Ti Jean! Where are you? Come back, I won't hurt you.

Nom: Hello, Jablotin. What's the problem? Why are you shouting?

Jablotin: *(angrily)* It's Ti Jean. He cheated me. He promised me I could pinch off a piece of his flesh if I beat him at cards. When I won the last game, he ran away and hid in the forest. When I find him, I will chop him into little pieces.

Nom: Calm down! I'll help you catch him. Let's make a plan.

Jablotin: What shall we do?

Nom: You must pretend to be dead. I will tell everyone and they will all come to your house to pay their last respects. When Ti Jean arrives, you can jump out and grab him. Then you can do what you want with him.

Jablotin: Thank you, Nom. You are a true friend. I will reward you when I catch Ti Jean.

Nom: Good. He will soon be yours.

Scene 2: At the market the next day

Nom: *(shouting)* Listen to me, everyone! Have you heard? Jablotin is dead.

Man: Oh no! When did that happen?

Nom: Last night, just after he went to bed. *(Ti Jean appears.)*

Man: Have you heard the news, Ti Jean? The monster Jablotin is dead. We're all going to his house to pay our last respects.

Ti Jean: Let me come with you. *(They all set off for Jablotin's house.)*

Scene 3: Outside Jablotin's house

Woman: So, Jablotin is dead at last! How did he die? Was it an accident?

Nom: No. A sudden fever killed him.

Ti Jean: *(in a loud voice)* Has he laughed since he died?

Nom: Shhh! *(whispering)* No, he hasn't!

Ti Jean: Then he can't be dead yet. Don't you know that when someone dies of fever, he must laugh a last big laugh?

Jablotin: *(from inside the house)* Ha ha ha!

Ti Jean: So, Jablotin, you are not dead after all. Don't you know that dead people can't laugh? Well, you'll never catch me! *(He runs away.)*

Jablotin: *(appearing in the doorway)* I'll get you one day, Ti Jean!

Nom: What about my reward?

Jablotin: *(furiously)* You don't deserve it. It's your fault that Ti Jean got away again. You are no friend of mine!

Comprehension

1 Where does the first scene take place?
2 What is Jablotin doing at the beginning of the first scene?
3 Why does Nom tell Jablotin to pretend to be dead?
4 What does 'to pay your last respects' mean?
5 Why do you think Nom whispers when he is outside Jablotin's house?
6 Is it true that when someone dies of a fever, he must laugh a big last laugh? Why do you think that Ti Jean says this?
7 How do you think Jablotin feels at the end of the play?
8 Do you think that Nom deserved to get a reward for helping Jablotin? Why? Why not?

Features of a play

The layout of a play includes the following features.
Scenes: the number of each scene and where it takes place
Names: of the characters speaking
Dialogue: the words the people say
Stage directions: instructions telling the actors what to do and how to speak

Identify these features in the play about Ti Jean and Jablotin.

Language | Contractions

Contractions are single words made up from two other words. We replace the missing letters with an apostrophe (').
Came back. I won't hurt you.
I won't is short for I will not.
We use contractions in informal speech and writing, We should not use contractions in formal speech or writing.

1 **Find five more examples of contractions in the play. Write them out in full.**

Example: It's Ti Jean.   *It is Ti Jean.*

2 **Write contractions for the following verbs.**

1 he is   *he's*
2 they were not
3 she is not

4 I did not
5 he does not
6 they are

7 I have not
8 it was not
9 he would

3 **Rewrite the conversation using contractions.**

Example: *"You're late," Ti Jean's wife told him.*

"You are late," Ti Jean's wife told him.

"I am sorry," Ti Jean replied. "I have got to go out again."

"We are all waiting for our dinner," Ti Jean's wife protested.

"I cannot stay," said Ti Jean. "You will have to eat without me. Do not worry. I will be back later."

"We do not want to eat without you. Why did you not tell me you were going out?"

"I will not be long," promised Ti Jean.

4 **Rewrite the review using full verb forms.**

I have
~~I've~~ just finished reading a play about Ti Jean. I hadn't read the play before. The story's about how Ti Jean tricks the monster Jablotin. I didn't think that Ti Jean would get away from Jablotin, but he's very cunning. Jablotin doesn't realise that Ti Jean's tricking him. In the end, Jablotin's only friend, Nom, isn't very happy because he hasn't received the reward he's expecting. We're going to act the play in class. I'm really looking forward to it.

Tricky words

It's or its?

It's is the short form of it is: It's a great book.

Its shows who or what owns something: Its author was born in Saint Lucia.

1 Complete the sentences with *it's* or *its*.

1 _____ time to get ready for the play.

2 I love the play. _____ first scene takes place in the forest.

3 Everyone went to Jablotin's house. _____ windows were open.

4 _____ very exciting performing in a play.

There, their or they're?

There tells us about place: Wait over there, please.

Their tells us who owns something: That is their house.

They're is the short form of *they are*: They're waiting outside.

2 Complete the sentences with *there, their* or *they're*.

1 Have the students learned _____ words for the play?

2 I told my parents and _____ coming to see the play.

3 I looked outside but I could not see anyone _____ .

4 The students are busy. _____ practising their play.

5 Who is playing Jablotin? Please stand over _____ .

6 Most students said that _____ parents would come to the play.

Words   Interjections

An **interjection** is a short word or phrase used to get people's attention or express strong feeling. It is followed by a **comma** or an **exclamation mark**.

Hey! Ti Jean.   Oh no, how did that happen?

1 Find the interjections in the following sentences.

1 <u>Hurry up!</u> You'll be late for the play.

2 Oh dear! I've forgotten my costume.

3 Good, I think we're all ready now.

4 Wow! You look amazing in your costume.

5 Shh! I can't hear what the actors are saying.

6 "Well done!" everyone said to the actors.

2 Complete the sentences with suitable interjections from the list below.

Ouch!   Shh!   Hooray!   Help!   Hey!   Oh no!

1 _____ Those are my shoes.
2 _____ I can't take off my costume.
3 _____ you just trod on my toe.
4 _____ I forgot my Mum's birthday.
5 _____ The holidays start tomorrow.
6 _____ Don't be so noisy.

3 Choose three interjections from the list above. Write them in your own sentences.

Hey! Those are my shoes.

Writing   Dialogue

⭐ **TASK:** Dramatise the first part of the play about Ti Jean and Jablotin.

1 Listen to the first part of the story again.

2 Plan your scene.
Note the events which happen in the correct sequence.

3 Write the first draft of your scene.
- Write where the scene takes place.
- Write the dialogue. Start like this:

Jablotin: Where are you going, Ti Jean?
Ti Jean: I'm going to the forest.

Remember to use stage directions telling the actors what to do and how to speak.

4 Discuss your first draft with another student. Revise it and make improvements.

5 Work in pairs. Act out your scene and your partner's scene.

6 Work in groups.
- Choose one of the first scenes written by group members.
- Choose students in the group to act the different parts.
- Act the whole play.

Before you read: Scan the text.

- What are the names of two well-known volcanoes?
- How many volcanoes are active each year?

Volcanoes

What is a volcano?

A volcano is a place where lava and gas erupt through the surface of the Earth. Lava is molten rock which becomes solid when it cools down. There are different types of volcanoes: some are just cracks in the ground, but others are cones with a crater at the top. Some volcanoes lie deep under the ocean floor. When a volcano erupts, it can cause great damage and loss of life.

Well-known volcanoes

Mount Vesuvius is in Italy. In 79 AD it erupted unexpectedly. The Roman city of Pompeii was buried under a thick layer of rock, mud and ash. No one had time to escape. Today thousands of people visit the site every year to see the ruins.

In 1883 the Indonesian volcano, Krakatoa, erupted. This was one of the biggest eruptions the world has ever known. It spread a huge cloud of dust right around the world and produced a 40 metre tsunami.

The Ruined City of Pompeii

Recent activity

Volcanoes can be active, dormant or extinct. About 60 volcanoes on land around the world are active each year, but there are many more active volcanoes under the sea. The Soufrière Hills in Monserrat is an active volcano. It started erupting in 1995, and forced the local population to leave the island.

Soufrière Hills

Mount Pelée in Martinique is a dormant volcano. Although it has not erupted for more than 100 years, it might erupt again one day. The underwater volcano, Kick-'Em Jenny, off the north coast of Grenada, is another dormant volcano. Scientists are keeping watch on it because they fear that it could one day produce a tsunami.

The Pitons on Saint Lucia are part of a volcano which last erupted thousands of years ago. The volcano is extinct, although there are still sulphur springs in the nearby town of Soufrière.

Glossary

erupt: send out rocks and gas in an explosion
lava: hot liquid rock that comes out of a volcano
molten: liquid
tsunami: a huge wave

Comprehension

1 How many different types of volcano are described in the first paragraph?
2 Which volcano is in Italy?
3 Why did no one escape when it erupted?
4 Which volcano produced an enormous wave when it erupted?
5 In which Caribbean islands can you find volcanoes?
6 Which Caribbean volcano is still active?
7 A dormant volcano is
  a a volcano that will never erupt again. **b** a volcano that might erupt again.
  c a volcano that has never erupted.
8 Why do volcanoes cause so much damage and loss of life?

Context

Select the correct definition for each underlined word. Use the context to help you.
1 The <u>origin</u> of the explosion is still unknown.
  a cause   **b** disaster   **c** problem
2 The huge eruption <u>compelled</u> many people to leave the island.
  a persuaded   **b** forced   **c** advised
3 Scientists are <u>concerned</u> that the volcano might produce a tsunami.
  a certain   **b** worried   **c** hopeful
4 The damage caused by a volcano erupting can be <u>considerable</u>.
  a minor   **b** unimportant   **c** very great

Stories

Before you read: Look at the picture.

Anansi and the Tug-of-War

Anansi was unhappy. The two biggest animals in the forest, Hippo and Elephant, laughed at him all the time. Anansi decided to play a trick on them.

He went to see Elephant. "Good morning, Elephant," he said. "You think you are very strong, but I am stronger than you. I challenge you to a Tug-of-War."

Elephant's great trunk shook with laughter. "No problem, little spider! I will win, that's for sure."

Anansi tied a rope around Elephant's tail. "When I shout, start pulling," he cried.

He raced off to the water hole, where Hippo was wallowing in the mud. He put the same challenge to Hippo, who agreed to the Tug-of-War. Anansi tied the other end of the rope around Hippo's fat belly. "When I shout, start pulling," he cried.

Anansi hid himself deep in the bushes and shouted, "Pull!" at the top of his voice.

There was silence for a moment, then Elephant roared and pulled Hippo right out of the mud. Hippo tugged on the rope and pulled Elephant through the forest. The trees crashed to the ground. The birds squawked and the monkeys squealed in fear.

The huge animals dragged and pulled, dragged and pulled until they were quite exhausted and collapsed on the ground. They were puzzled. How could the tiny spider be so strong?

Then Anansi leapt out of the bushes. "Who is stronger?" he cried as he jumped on the Elephant's trunk.

"You are," sighed Elephant.

"Who is stronger?" he cried as he jumped on the Hippo's nose.

"You are," gasped Hippo.

Read a traditional story.

Comprehension

1 How did Anansi feel at the beginning of the story?
2 Why did he feel like that?
3 What challenge did he give to Elephant?
4 How did Elephant feel about the challenge?
   a nervous   **b** unwilling   **c** amused
5 Where was Hippo when Anansi went to speak to him?
6 Why were Hippo and Elephant puzzled when the Tug-of-War ended?
7 How do you think Anansi felt at the end of the story?

Copy and complete the story chart about 'Anansi and the Tug-of-War'.

Characters	
Setting	
Problem	
Events	
Ending	

Language Verbs

1 Complete the sentences with verbs in the present perfect tense.

has caused
1 The lava from the volcano (**cause**) a lot of damage.
2 We (**visit**) the Sulphur Springs a few times.
3 I (**take**) a lot of photos of the Pitons.
4 My uncle (**go**) to Martinique.
5 My cousin (**write**) me a letter about his trip.

2 Write what everyone was doing at the botanical gardens yesterday.
Use the past continuous tense.

Example: children + listen to guide   The children were listening to a guide.

1 I + take pictures
2 my mother + look at flowers
3 my grandmother + sit in shade
4 my friends + eat ice cream
5 my brother + swim in hot pool
6 birds + perch in trees

3 **Rewrite the dialogue using contractions.**

We're going

Marie: ~~We are going~~ to the Sulphur Springs tomorrow.

Tim: I have not been there. I would like to see them. Can I come with you?

Marie: Our car is not very big, I do not think there will be enough room.

Tim: That does not matter. I will go another time.

Marie: It is a very interesting place. I will tell you all about it.

Tim: I am looking forward to hearing about it.

Marie: My father is calling me. I must not be late. Bye!

Prepositions

1 **Find five different prepositions in the story 'Anansi and the Tug-of-War'.**

2 **Complete the sentences with suitable prepositions from the list below.**

at around from in under up for to

1 The last time the volcano erupted was _____ 1995.
2 The ash from the volcano spread right _____ the world.
3 There are a lot of volcanoes _____ the sea.
4 Some volcanoes have not erupted _____ thousands of years.
5 The guide told us to move away _____ the crater.
6 My uncle plans to climb right _____ to the top of Gros Piton.
7 We are going _____ the Botanical Gardens tomorrow.
8 The tour will start _____ 2:00 p.m.

Joining sentences

1 **Complete the sentences with *which, who* or *where*.**

1 A volcano is a place _____ lava breaks through the Earth's surface.
2 The emergency services rescued the people _____ were trapped.
3 The houses _____ were damaged in the earthquake have been repaired.
4 We listened carefully to the guide _____ showed us around.
5 We walked to the place _____ the bus was waiting for us.
6 The guide took us to the pool _____ smelt like rotten eggs.

Revise contractions, prepositions and relative pronouns.

2 **Join the sentences with *because* or *although*.**

Example: We had to wait a long time because the bus was late.

We had to wait a long time.		The bus was late.
Mike went up to the crater.		The guide told him not to.
Volcanoes cause a lot of damage.	**because**	The lava can bury a town.
We did not swim today.		The water was too cold.
I enjoyed visiting the crater.	**although**	It smelt bad there.
There is a volcano in Martinique.		It has not erupted recently.

Words **Homographs**

1 **Write the part of speech of each underlined homograph.**

1 The <u>stick</u> is broken. I want to <u>stick</u> it together. noun / verb
2 Can you see the <u>sign</u>? This is where we must <u>sign</u> our names.
3 We will <u>paint</u> the wall with this blue <u>paint</u>.
4 Is your new <u>flat</u> on a hill or on <u>flat</u> ground?
5 <u>Duck</u> your head when you go under the bridge. There is a <u>duck</u> in the water.
6 There is a <u>cross</u> on the map at the point where you <u>cross</u> the road.

2 **Write your own sentences using the homographs as different parts of speech.**

1 patient (**noun / adjective**)   4 cold (**noun / adjective**)
2 park (**noun / verb**)   5 wave (**noun / verb**)
3 show (**noun / verb**)   6 light (**noun / adjective**)

Compound nouns

Match the words in Column A and Column B to make compound nouns.

Example: suit + case = suitcase

Column A	Column B
suit	storm
thunder	guard
neck	ache
tooth	case
life	lace

Column A	Column B
tea	stairs
house	work
down	cloth
sun	spoon
table	set

Study Skills Graphs

Study the information in the graph. Answer the questions.

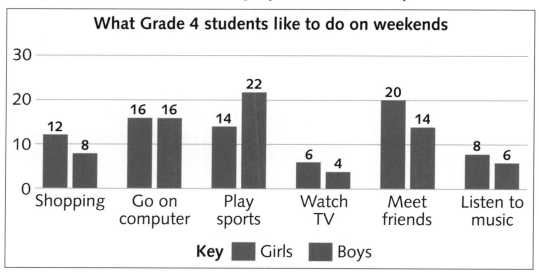

What Grade 4 students like to do on weekends

Key ▮ Girls ▮ Boys

1 Which is the most popular activity for boys?
2 Which activity is liked by the same number of girls and boys?
3 Which activity is least popular with both boys and girls?
4 Which activity do the girls like most?
5 How many boys like going shopping?
6 Which activity do you like to do best on weekends? Explain why.

Using a thesaurus

Study the extracts from a thesaurus.

> **happy:** cheerful, contented, delighted, pleased, satisfied, thrilled

> **sad:** depressed, disappointed, gloomy, sorry, unhappy, upset

Use words to replace _happy_ and _sad_ in these sentences.
1 Carl is always <u>happy</u> even when things are difficult for him.
2 Dana was <u>sad</u> when her best friend was unkind to her.
3 Michael was <u>sad</u> when his favourite team lost their match.
4 Paulette was <u>happy</u> when she won the prize for the best reader.
5 Ben's teacher was <u>happy</u> with his progress in class.
6 After they lost their match, the cricketers felt <u>sad</u>.

Writing

⭐ TASK 1: Write a report about one of the following topics.

- My school
- The place where I live

1 **GETTING IDEAS**

Brainstorm with another student information about the topic you chose.
Use question words to help you.

What?   **Where?**   **When?**   **Who?**   **Why?**   **How?**

2 **PLANNING**

Write a heading and make notes for each section of your report.

Example:

My school	
Where it is	
Who goes there	
What we learn there	

3 Write the first draft of your report.

Remember to divide the information into paragraphs.

4 Revise your first draft. Check it carefully and write a neat copy.

⭐ TASK 2: Write a story about an animal that solved a difficult problem.

1 **PLANNING**

Complete a story plan about your animal.

Setting and characters	
Problem	
Events	
How problem was solved	

2 **DRAFTING**

Write the first draft of your story. Revise it and write a neat copy.

Listening Scripts

Unit 1

Mrs. Samuel: (*clapping her hands to get the students' attention*) Listen to me, students. I have heard your presentations and I have chosen two students to give their presentations to the class. Kim, will you go first, please?

Kim: Yes, Miss. My cousins from the USA came to stay. We had a great time. We met them at Hewanorra Airport. We got there early so we could watch their plane land. Then we went into the airport building and waited for them to go through customs and immigration. It took a really long time. At last we saw my uncle pushing a trolley with their luggage. My aunt and my cousins, Brad and Melanie, were behind him. Then we all got into a big taxi and drove home. We went to the beach every day and one day my uncle hired a boat and we went fishing. We took them to Pigeon Point and the Sulphur Springs at Soufrière. I was really sad when they went home.

Mrs. Samuel: Does anyone have any questions for Kim?

Luke: Yes, I do. Did your cousins bring you any gifts from the USA?

Kim: They brought gifts for the whole family. They gave Mum and Dad a new tablet computer, and I had a little camera. I will bring it to school one day and take pictures of everyone.

Mrs. Samuel: Thank you, Kim. You spoke really well. Now it's Luke's turn.

Unit 2

Sound of phone ringing

Shanice: Hello. This is Shanice speaking. Is that Mrs. Charles?

Mrs. Charles: Yes, it is. Would you like to speak to Dana?

Shanice: Yes, please.

Mrs. Charles: Just a moment…

Dana: Hello! Is that Shanice?

Shanice: Yes, it is. Dana, I've got some exciting news. It's the Feast of La Marguerite on Saturday. Mum is taking me to see the parade in Castries. She says I can bring a friend, so I'm asking you.

Dana: That would be great. I've never been to the parade before.

Shanice: I went last year. Everyone was dressed in blue and white. Each community carried its own banner. The day started with a church service. Then the parade set off around the city. In the evening they had the *grande fête*.

Dana: What is that?

Shanice: It's a big party which starts with a feast. People dance traditional dances like the *kwadril* and the *mappa* until late at night.

Dana: Will we go to the *grande fête* this year?

Shanice: No, we'll just watch the parade. Then Mum will take us for a meal.

Dana: I'd love to come. Thanks for asking me.

Unit 3

Storyteller: Jason was really looking forward to his ninth birthday. His Mum and Dad had promised him a great party with cake, balloons, party games – the works. Jason wrote the invitation list himself. He tried not to leave out any of his friends.

As the day drew nearer, everyone was talking about Jason's party. His Mum bought the ingredients to make him a special birthday cake. John knew that this party was going to be the best ever.

Finally the great day arrived. Jason's Mum served him breakfast in bed and wished him happy birthday. Then she began to decorate the house. Soon Jason's aunt arrived with a basket full of delicious cakes. Jason's aunt laid the table and his Mum put the drinks on ice. John helped his Dad blow up the balloons.

By two o'clock everything was ready. The party guests were due to arrive at three. Jason was getting impatient. He could not wait for the party to start.

All of a sudden the sky turned charcoal black. There was a loud thunderclap and lightning lit up the sky. Then the heaviest rain Jason had ever seen began to fall. "My party is ruined," he muttered to himself.

Unit 4

Radio host: Good evening, listeners, and welcome to Sports Review. Let's hear from athletics coach Lester James. We have a quite a lot of promising athletes in Saint Lucia now, don't we?

Coach: Yes, that's right. High jumper Darvin Edwards is one of them. I think that he is one of Saint Lucia's finest athletes.

Host: What can you tell us about his career?

Coach: He was born in Castries in 1986 and went to school there. While he was at the Entrepot Secondary School he was spotted by coach Gregory Lubin, who trained him in high jump. His first big success was in 2004 when he won the Under-20 men's high jump at the CARIFTA Games in Bermuda. Two years later he was selected for the Commonwealth Games in Australia in 2006.

Host: Has he always trained in Saint Lucia?

Coach: No, after the games in Australia he went to England to train for a few months. After that, he set a new record for Saint Lucia. However, he suffered a serious back injury in 2009 and was out of action for a whole year.

Host: He made a come-back after that though, didn't he?

Coach: Oh yes, he worked hard to overcome his injury. Since then he has competed in games around the world, including the London Olympics in 2012.

Host: What is the highest he has ever jumped?

Coach: His personal best is 231 metres. That is the OECS record.

Host: I think that we Saint Lucians can be really proud of him.

Unit 5

The Hen

The hen is a ferocious fowl,
She pecks you till she makes you howl.

And all the time she flaps her wings,
And says the most insulting things.

And when you try to take her eggs,
She bites large pieces from your legs.

The only safe way to get these
Is to crawl on your hands and knees.

In the meanwhile a friend must hide,
And jump out on the other side.

And then you snatch the eggs and run,
While she pursues the other one.

The difficulty is, to find
A trusty friend who will not mind.

Unit 6

Radio announcer: There's an exciting weekend ahead for the residents of Coral Bay. Not to be missed is St. Joseph's Church Annual Fish Fry, taking place on the beach itself, from 6:00 p.m. onwards. There will be freshly grilled fish of all sorts including mahi mahi and tuna. All the fish will be caught that day by our local fishermen. Come and eat your fill for $25; kids, for just $10. Then from 8 o'clock, there will be music from the Starlight Band for you to dance until late, late, late. Get your tickets in advance from the church office or buy them when you arrive. Get set for an evening of fun!

Unit 7

Storyteller: One day Anansi picked some fat, tasty yams from his garden. He baked them with care and they smelt delicious. He could not wait to eat them. Just then he heard a knock at his door. It was Turtle. He had been travelling all day. He was very tired and hungry.

"Hello, Anansi," said Turtle. "I am very tired. Please may I share your meal?"

It was the custom in Anansi's country to share your meal with visitors so Anansi could not refuse. He was not happy. He wanted the yams all to himself. He thought for a moment.

"Please come in, Turtle. Sit down and help yourself."

Just as Turtle reached for a yam, Anansi yelled, "Turtle, don't you know better than to come to the table with dirty hands?"

Turtle looked down at his hands. They were filthy. He went down to the river to clean them. Then he walked all the way back up to the house. Anansi had already begun to eat. Turtle sat down again and reached for a yam, but again Anansi yelled at him.

"Turtle, did you not hear me before? It is not polite to come to the table with dirty hands!"

Turtle looked down and saw that his clean hands were dirty again as he had crawled on them back to the house. So he walked down to the river again to wash. When he returned this time, he walked on the grass so his hands would stay clean. But by the time he sat down at the table, Anansi had finished the last bit of the tasty yams and there was not so much as a morsel left.

Unit 8

Guide: Good morning, students, and welcome to the Union Nature Trail. My name is Jackson, and I am your guide for the day. I work for the Forestry Department. We have a lot of beautiful forests in Saint Lucia and we need to look after them. However, we are losing our forests because people are cutting down trees for firewood and using them to build houses and make furniture. The Forestry Department is trying to protect our forests. Our motto is 'La Fowey et Terre Se La Vie'.

Today we are going to walk on a trail through the forest. I will show you lots of things on the way. We will be around an hour and a half on the trail. If we are lucky we will see some of the birds that live in the forest, like hummingbirds, finches and parrots. Then I will take you to the mini-zoo. You will see some of the animals which are native to Saint Lucia, like the Saint Lucia parrot, the boa and the agouti. We have a small collection of animals from other countries too, such as macaws and green monkeys.

It will be quite hot on the way, so make sure you have plenty of water with you. Do not step off the trail when we are in the forest. Is everyone ready?... Then follow me.

Unit 9

Waves

There are big waves and little waves,
Green waves and blue,
Waves you can jump over,
Waves you dive through,
Waves that rise up
Like a great water wall,
Waves that swell softly
And don't break at all,
Waves that can whisper,
Waves that can roar,
And tiny waves that run at you
Running on the shore.

Unit 10

Brandon: Good morning, Mrs. Alexander. Good morning, students. For my invention, I chose the aeroplane. I think that it is wonderful that today

we can fly all around the world, don't you? It used to take days to travel from one place to another. Now we can get there in a few hours, thanks to the invention of the aeroplane.

The first plane was invented just over 100 years ago by the Wright brothers, who lived in the USA. They owned a bicycle shop, but in their spare time, they were inventors. In 1903 they made their first flight in a motorised plane. It lasted just a few seconds. They made some improvements and by the following year, they were able to stay in the air for nearly one hour.

Soon planes could fly quite long distances. In 1927 Charles Lindbergh became the first man to fly solo across the Atlantic Ocean. The journey from New York to Paris took him 33 hours. A modern passenger plane can cover this distance in seven hours.

Today planes can stay in the air for more than 15 hours. The latest passenger planes carry up to 600 passengers. They fly at a height of more than seven miles above the surface of the Earth at a speed of 500 miles an hour. I do not think that even the Wright brothers could have imagined the way that air travel has turned out today.

Unit 11

Storyteller: Jaydon was small for his age, and he was tired of the other boys teasing him about his size. He decided to play a trick on them. Soon it would be his birthday. He planned a special party to which only the boys who teased him would be invited. "If I can get them to come to my party, I will scare them to death," he said.

On the day of Jaydon's party, his guests found a note at the door. "Please come in," it said. The boys opened the door and saw a huge plastic skeleton hanging from the ceiling. "Oooh! This place is creepy," said one of the boys.

Jaydon had closed the curtains so the room was very dark. There were ghostly figures hanging from the lights. The boys were scared. Then they heard a loud, ghostly voice calling them. It was Jaydon, who was standing on a table, wrapped in a white sheet. He was holding a bucket over his head.

"This bucket is full of worms," he told the boys. "You must promise to stop teasing me, or I will throw the worms at you."

"We promise," the boys said quickly.

"That's good," said Jaydon. "Now let's party!" He jumped off the table and showed the boys what was in the bucket. It was full of popcorn.

Unit 12

Jessica: Hey, Mark. How are you doing?

Mark: Hi, Jessica. I'm feeling good. How about you?

Jessica: Not so good! This uniform is so uncomfortable. I think it's about time we stopped wearing uniforms to school.

Mark: But, Jessica, uniforms are a good thing.

Jessica: What is so good about them? You wear the same thing every day.

Mark: Uniforms give us an identity. When people see us in our uniforms they know which school we attend.

Jessica: I don't really care about that! Why can't we wear what we want? I like to choose what I wear.

Mark: Jessica! You should be proud of your school and wearing your uniform says who you are.

Jessica: I am proud of my school. I just don't like wearing a uniform.

Mark: The uniform also helps our parents save money. They have fewer clothes to buy for us. Some parents have lots of money to spend on clothes, others do not. If we wear uniform no one will know the difference.

Jessica: All of what you said is true. I guess I don't have a choice but to wear it.

Unit 13

Officer Charles: Good morning, students. I am Forest Officer Charles and I work for the Saint Lucia National Trust. I am going to tell you about the Maria Islands. The islands are located off the south coast of Saint Lucia, close to the town of Vieux Fort. The islands are a nature reserve. They are a protected wildlife area as some very special reptiles live there. That means that people cannot visit the islands on their own. You need to get permission from the National Trust.

Two of the reptiles, the Saint Lucia whiptail lizard and the Saint Lucia racer snake, are only found on the Maria Islands.

The whiptail is a small blue, black and yellow lizard. It lives mainly on the ground, but sometimes it climbs trees. It feeds on insects, flowers and fruits, and small sea creatures and fish which have been washed up from the sea.

The racer is the world's rarest snake. We think that there are fewer than 20 of them left. The racer is light brown in colour. It lives on the ground and feeds on lizards, birds and frogs.

Unit 14

Listen to Fire Officer 391 Davis telling the students of Saint John's Primary School what to do in case of fire.

Fire Officer Davis: Good morning, students. Fires do not happen often in schools, but you need to know what to do in case of a fire in your classroom or school. That is why we have fire drills. Listen carefully to the fire drill procedure.

When you hear the fire alarm:

STOP what you are doing at once and wait quietly.
LISTEN carefully to your teacher's directions.
LEAVE your things on your desk.
LINE UP at the door in silence.
WALK to the assembly area. Don't run.
WAIT with your classmates while your teacher calls the roll.
DO NOT RE-ENTER the building until your teacher tells you it is safe to do so.

Unit 15

News announcer: Fire has destroyed the church hall at Palm View Heights. The fire broke out between 7:00 and 8:00 p.m. last Sunday evening. A passer-by saw flames rising from the roof and immediately called the Fire Service.

Firemen were on the scene within 20 minutes, but it was too late to save the building. It took the firemen two hours to bring the fire under control. One of the firemen suffered minor injuries. He has been admitted to hospital in Castries. Luckily, no one was inside the hall when the fire broke out.

The cause of the fire is not yet known. The caretaker of the church hall told our reporter that groups of boys often meet behind the hall for the popular pastime of bamboo bursting. "I'm always telling them to stay away from the building," he said, "but they don't listen to me. Maybe they spilt some kerosene and that set light to the hall. It's a wooden building so it burned down quickly." The Chief of the Fire Service does not agree with this theory. He thinks that an electrical fault caused the fire.

Unit 16

This is an announcement from the Saint Lucia Solid Waste Management Authority.

Hello, kids, this is Tin Tin. I have an important message for you. Do you know that when you throw garbage in the streets it blocks the drains and leads to flooding? It attracts flies and is a health risk too.

So play your part in keeping your community clean. Here's what you can do:

Make sure your trash goes in the garbage bin, not just near it.

Pick up litter from around your home and school.

If you see your friends dropping trash, tell them to put it in the bin.

Clear up after a picnic on the beach or in the park.

Don't throw trash out of the bus window.

Garbage can take hundreds of years to rot away, so LET'S GO GREEN!

Unit 17

Announcer: Good morning, everyone, and welcome to our radio call-in show, 'What's on Your Mind?' It's time for our first caller, Mr. Kelvin James. So, Mr. James, what's on your mind?

Mr. James: I'm very concerned about sand mining. It's against the law in Saint Lucia, but every day people are taking sand from our beaches to build their houses or for other forms of construction. Thousands of cubic yards of sand are lost from our beaches every year. This is destroying the habitat of much of the wildlife on our island. The iguana lays its eggs in the sand. When people remove the sand, they destroy the young iguanas which are developing there. Leatherback turtles also lay their eggs in the sand along our east coast. They are an endangered species. If people continue taking sand, the leatherback will soon become extinct.

Announcer: So sand mining is threatening our wildlife?

Mr. James: Yes, but that is not all. The tourist industry is very important in Saint Lucia. People come from all over the world to enjoy our sunshine and beautiful beaches. If people keep taking the sand, the beaches will be ruined. If this happens, the tourists will stop coming. Hundreds of people who depend on the tourist industry will be out of a job.

Announcer: Thank you, Mr. James. Now, listeners, it's your turn. If you have any ideas about how to stop illegal sand mining, call the radio station on 459 7214.

Unit 18

Storyteller: Jablotin was an evil monster. For a long time, he had been trying to eat his neighbour, Ti Jean. He tried all sorts of tricks, but Ti Jean always managed to escape.

One day Ti Jean set out for the forest. Jablotin saw him and asked him if he wanted to play cards. Ti Jean asked what they would play for. Jablotin told him that they would play for fun. He added that the winner could pinch off a bit of flesh from the loser.

Ti Jean knew what Jablotin was up to, but he still agreed to play. He told Jablotin that he was going home first to speak to his wife. While he was at home, he fetched his own pack of cards, for he knew that Jablotin would try to cheat.

Sure enough, when he returned, Ti Jean's sharp eyes spotted two cards poking out of Jablotin's pocket. He checked the cards on the table and slipped in two of his own to replace the cards Jablotin had removed.

They began to play and Ti Jean won the first game. He told Jablotin that he did not want to pinch off any of his flesh. Jablotin was very surprised. He thought Ti Jean must be either very generous, or stupid. They went on playing and Ti Jean kept on winning. Jablotin became furious.

"You must be cheating!" he shouted.

At last Jablotin won a game. He was delighted. "Now I can pinch off your whole arm, Ti Jean," he roared.

Ti Jean leapt up and raced into the woods as fast as his legs could carry him. Jablotin ran after him, but Ti Jean was nowhere to be seen.

Index

Macmillan Education
4 Crinan Street
London, N1 9XW
A division of Springer Nature Limited
Companies and representatives throughout the world

www.macmillan-caribbean.com

ISBN 978-0-230-48117-6

Designed by Clare Webber
Illustrated by: Heather Clarke; Plum Pudding Illustration: Gabby Grant & Sue King; Beehive Illustration: Robin Lawrie & Matt Ward;
Sylvie Poggio Artists: Monica Auriemma, Humberto Blanco, Tony Forbes, Bethan Mathews, Lisa Williams, Paul Williams;
Tech Type; Blue Dog Design Studio.
Cover design by Clare Webber
Cover illustration by David Dean
Typesetting and art buying by Blue Dog Design Studio

The publishers would like to thank Julia Sander for her contribution.

The author and publisher would like to thank the following for permission to reproduce the following material.
Poem 'The Donkey' by Gertrude Hind, copyright © Punch Ltd 1927. Reprinted by permission of Punch Ltd. Further commercial
reproduction of this material is prohibited without prior consent. All enquiries to info@punch.co.uk, www.punch.co.uk
Poem 'There are Big Waves' by Eleanor Farjeon, copyright © Eleanor Farjeon, from 'Blackbird Has Spoken: Selected Poems for Children',
Macmillan Children's Books 2000. Reprinted by permission of David Higham Associates on behalf of the estate of Eleanor Farjeon.

These materials may contain links for third party websites. We have no control over, and are not responsible for, the contents of such
third party websites. Please use care when accessing them.

The authors and publishers would like to thank the following for permission to reproduce their photographs:
Germain Anthony pp 46, 58, 59(t), 95, 101, 112; **Zenith Edward** p17; **Getty Images** p130(tr), Getty Images/iStockphoto/Thinkstock
Images/koya79 p71(b), Getty Images/iStockphoto/Thinkstock /Oleksiy Mark p72(b), Getty Images/iStockphoto/Thinkstock Images/
UmbertoPantalone p72(t), Getty Images/Chris McGrath p28; **Johnson James** p16; **Macmillan Publishers Ltd.** pp 20, 59(b), p94;
Matthew Morton/Gregory Guida p96; **PhotoDisc/Getty Images** pp 71(t), 92; **Rex/Shutterstock/Robert Perry** p29; **Saint Lucia
Solid Waste Management Authority** p112(b); **Shutterstock/Adrian Reynold**s p130 (br); **Thinkstock**/iStock/Lidian Neeleman p12

Printed and bound in Great Britain by Bell & Bain Ltd, Glasgow
2021 2020 2019
10 9 8 7 6 5 4